Management Accounting Systems and Records

Management Accounting Systems and Records

Bob Grimsley

Second edition by **M. W. Monaghan**

Gower

First published 1972
Reprinted 1978, 1979
Second edition 1981
© Gower Publishing Company Limited 1981

Published by
Gower Publishing Company Limited
Aldershot, Hants, England.
Printed and bound in Great Britain
at The Pitman Press, Bath.

 British Library Cataloguing in Publication Data

Grimsley, Bob
    Management accounting systems and records — 2nd ed.
    1. Accounting
    I. Title   II. Monaghan, M. W.
    651.5   HF5635

    ISBN 0-566-02349-0

Contents

Illustrations

Introduction

The records in this book are intended to be used by managers. Each manager must understand the words and figures being served up to him and if the presentation is not clear and obvious the system has failed in its job.

Management accounting is a tool for use by all kinds of management, not merely accountants. It is the presentation of facts to show past results which help in the preparation of forecasts for the future. The tool places managers in a position to act with confidence for the strong control of their company, yet in no way does it supplant the need for managers to keep the control or to initiate the action personally.

It is the responsibility of the accountant to help set up a system suitable to his company, to explain it to the other executives and to keep it running smoothly. If the executives ignore or misunderstand the system the company is the loser because the opportunity for strong control is being wasted and this is even more serious than the expense of running the management accounting to no purpose.

The subject centres largely around the idea that the purpose of running the business is to make a profit — highest long-term net profit. Measurement of total income, and of the various ways this has been modified through purchases and expenses to arrive at the final result, is a basic part of the work. The main subdivisions of the subject are shown by the chapter headings. Two terms call for explanation:

1   *Budgetary control* is defined by the Institute of Cost and Management Accountants as: the establishment of budgets relating the responsibility of executives to the requirements of a policy, and the continuous comparison of actual with budgeted results, either to secure individual action to achieve the objective of the policy, or to provide a basis for its revision

2   *Accounting ratios*. A ratio is the relationship of one set of facts or figures to another set, reduced to a percentage or fraction. The purpose of accounting

ratios is to enable managers to make financial comparisons of like with like, with past performance, with future expectations, with competitors and with national averages

Both budgetary control and accounting ratios are such basic parts of management accounting that they crop up in every chapter instead of being isolated in chapters of their own.

The aim in this book is to produce a practical working guide for business managers. From the general guide it is always necessary to tailor the systems and records to fit the individual business because each company is unique.

The Computer in Management Accounting

A computer will store information, accept fresh information, do arithmetic and print out many of the management accounting records. It will enable a firm to produce the records more quickly (subject to availability of operating staff) and with a greater variety of analyses.

Thus a computer is a tool for use in the management accounting function which, in turn, is a tool of management. It does not cancel the need for the systems and records, described in the following chapters, although it may produce them in a different shape and produce them more quickly. Nor does the fact that it can turn out complex sheets of figures mean that such sheets are better for the management. The simple straightforward presentation of key figures is equally important whether or not the company has a computer at its disposal. The figures remain useful only to the extent that the managers are themselves capable of interpreting what is shown.

Current Cost Accounting

Following considerable debate extending over many years and a number of false starts, an accounting standard, SSAP 16, was issued in 1980 entitled Current Cost Accounting. The stated objective was to provide more useful information than that available from historical cost accounts alone. To achieve this three main adjustments to the accounts are required: (i) depreciation adjustment (ii) cost of sales adjustment and (iii) monetary working capital adjustment.

These adjustments allow for the impact of price changes, although CCA is not a system of accounting for general inflation.

Although not applicable to the wholly owned subsidiaries of a UK registered parent, in general the Standard applies to entities with

1   An annual turnover of £5 million or more
2   A balance sheet total of not less than £2.5 million and
3   An average number employed of not less than 250

Those companies to which the Standard applies may still publish historical cost accounts as the main accounts, with current cost accounts provided in supplementary form. Companies using current cost accounts as the main accounts are still required to supply adequate historical cost information.

The accounting policies should be the same for both systems and the same tools of analysis, ratios etc., described in this book, are generally appropriate.

1

Monthly Accounts

Monthly accounts are used to check progress at regular intervals. Basically they resemble annual accounts but they enable the management to check the company's progress at frequent intervals instead of waiting a whole year.

Some companies content themselves with quarterly accounts, but these are a poor substitute because a great deal can happen in competitive industry in the space of three months. Others favour fortnightly or even weekly accounts which are excellent if they can be produced accurately and quickly without undue expense. Essentials are:

1   *Simplicity.* It is better to have the main facts set out clearly than to have a lot of elaborate complications
2   *Speed.* Each day spent in preparation cuts down the benefit obtainable from these short-term records
3   *Accuracy.* Perfect accuracy may fairly be sacrificed for the sake of speed, provided that the margin of error is understood. Each firm should work out its own tolerances to reach a reasonable compromise
4   *Detail.* Departmental detail should be set out clearly for departmental managers to use. Summaries should go forward to the central management supported by copies of the detailed sheets

A budget should have been made before the start of each month. The monthly accounts will show the actual results compared to the budget. Some companies also like to make a comparison with the equivalent month in the preceding year, but this is a matter of personal choice and, in financial terms, has lost some of its relevance because of inflation. It is rather in the preparation of the budget that the preceding year's figures are likely to be of most use.

Every manager is likely to be concerned with some aspect of the month's results but it will not be necessary for most of them to see more than relates to their own department. Each chapter in this book will suggest the distribution of accounts to managers in a typical manufacturing business. However, it should be noted that each company must work out for itself which of its executives should receive which of the accounts.

Each manager should look on it as his own responsibility to see that his share of the accounts is prepared regularly and promptly. This will be the case even in the larger company where specialist staff are engaged in the work. For example, if a departmental production manager normally receives three completed sheets by the third day of each month and one month they fail to appear, he should inquire for them on that day rather than wait an impatient week for them to turn up. If he does not fret at their absence or does not even notice, this is proof that he has not been in the habit of using the accounts properly.

In this chapter the specimen forms are presented in reverse order from the way they would be created. The master sheets intended for central management are shown first, followed by the detailed sheets from which the masters have been built up.

Graphs

For those who like the graphic representation to give a quick impression of the main facts, a variety of graphs may be devised. However, it should be realised that a graph is not a substitute for a careful study of the accounts, particularly where those accounts are showing some unsatisfactory feature of the business. Figure 1:1 is an example of a graph used in accounting.

Monthly Manufacturing Accounts

The function of the manufacturing account is to draw together all the direct costs of making the goods, with the fixed and variable expenses of running the factory in which they are made.

By showing quantities as well as figures, it draws attention to rise and fall in the volume of output as well as in value. This information is useful in itself and can be extended to show the changing costs per unit of the product.

The account has isolated the costs of the factory, which is under the control of the factory manager, from the costs of selling and of administration, which are under other authority and appear in the profit and loss account.

Master sheet for the manufacturing account

Figure 1:2 shows an example of a master sheet for the manufacturing account. No figure is shown for the more detailed review of direct expenses because these vary so much from one business to another. The pattern for analysing them would be similar to that for Figure 1:3.

The costs of making goods are isolated from the costs of trading in finished goods and from general administrative expenses. Prime cost is a key figure because it includes only those costs which result directly from what has been made during the period, whereas factory costs would have continued with different levels of production although possibly the amount could be different.

It is important to include quantity as well as money because price changes could obscure the true level of production. The unit of measurement to use may be a puzzle if the nature of the finished product is very different from the ingredients of the raw materials. The solution is to use against prime cost the unit applicable to finished goods and have the quantity of raw material covered as in Figure 1:3.

A margin of profit for the factory may be added to the total of factory costs to arrive at the figure to be transferred to the trading account. The benefits of this system are discussed in Chapter 2. Many firms settle the amount of profit by taking an agreed percentage of the factory costs, but this has all the drawbacks of the cost-plus system which shows a greater profit when there has been inefficient and extravagant control of the business. The better plan is to make the total transferred to the account 'not more than £x per completed unit'.

In a company which has more than one factory it is important to distinguish between their results. To make separate manufacturing accounts for each factory is recommended, with a summary of the key figures of prime cost and factory costs to show their combined results.

Raw material in manufacturing account

Figure 1:3 shows an example of an account of raw material in manufacturing. According to the nature of the product, the summary by types of process may be used alternatively or additionally to the summary by departments. Loss in value of material may be caused by a sharp drop in market prices, wastage because of faulty manufacturing, theft, fire or other calamity. These must be the subject of a separate entry on the account sheet after the main departments but before the total. Explanatory notes should be added at the foot of the page.

Sales of scrap material correctly arising in the natural process of the manufacture should be deducted from this raw material account and only the net total carried to the main manufacturing account. This should be distinguished from sales of scrapped completed goods which are wasted by faulty manufacture. Wastage of this kind should be plainly set out on the main manufacturing account so that management may take steps to ensure that the faults are not repeated.

Direct wages in manufacturing account

Figure 1:3 shows an example of an account of direct wages in manufacturing. Man-hours is the most usual unit of measurement of quantity of labour but some firms adopt other standards. An overall picture of wages may mask several oddities which should be revealed by a more detailed analysis such as is described in Chapter 7.

Work in progress

Work in progress is shown in the form illustrated in Figure 1:4. In practice the accurate measurement of work in progress is very difficult and poor guesses are a cause of monthly accounts being inaccurate. For most factories the holding of some work in progress is inevitable. When material goes through successive stages of processing it may be desirable to keep a buffer stock of partly processed material ready to go into each stage of production. Production managers should set target levels of work in progress rather than adopt the attitude that the lowest level must be the best level. Any variation beyond the acceptable x per cent tolerance from the target level calls for detailed queries. It is costly and inefficient to hold excessive amounts of work in progress and may be specially dangerous where the product could go out of fashion or deteriorate in value for some other reason.

In some companies, incidentally, a proportion of the cost of overheads is added to wages and material to arrive at the value of work in progress. These are usually an arbitrary fixed percentage anywhere between nil and the full percentage that overheads bear to prime costs over all productions. This is very dangerous, however. The true relation of production overheads to prime cost may vary widely between products and because of changes in production techniques the relation of any product may vary from year to year.

Indirect wages in factory costs

Figure 1:5 illustrates an example of a cost statement of indirect wages in the factory. There may be many kinds of indirect workers; care should be taken that all are entered, including the suitable proportion of wages for employees whose work is partly indirectly and partly directly productive. Apprentices and working foremen and supervisors are likely to be in this group. Chapter 5 gives further details on the balancing of wages.

The specimen account for salaries would closely resemble the one for indirect wages. It is likely to include the factory manager and his assistants and the production departmental manager, the cost and records clerks, time clerks and time study staff. Care should be taken that everyone receiving a salary appears in this list or in one of the lists attached to the profit and loss account.

Machinery in factory costs

Figure 1:6 illustrates the form used to show the costs of machinery in a factory. Only factory machinery is included in this summary. Office machinery and dispatch warehouse machinery will be included in the appropriate section of the profit and loss account. Wages for maintenance engineers have been included in the indirect factory wages analysis and must not be repeated here. Some firms, however, prefer to enter them with the machinery costs and leave them out of the indirect wages.

The nature of depreciation as a cost is quite different from the running and upkeep expenses because it has no place in the outwards cash flow statement. In addition, the true measure of depreciation is not known in any single short period and the figures to be entered here would be based on informed opinion rather than an exact statement of the amount by which the machinery has actually worn out. Depreciation may be taken at an annual percentage based on the original cost price of the machine. This is known as the fixed instalment or straight-line method. It may be further improved by estimating the number of productive working hours of the life of the machine and so arriving at a fairly accurate cost of depreciation per hour, worked during the period covered by the month's accounts.

The straight-line method is suitable for machines the production capacity of which remains fairly steady throughout their working lives and which do not incur heavy expense and loss of working hours because of major repairs during the later stages. The reducing balance or diminishing instalment method of depreciation takes a higher percentage but calculates afresh each year on the written-down value instead of the original cost price. The effect is to load depreciation more heavily in the early years. This is ideal for a machine which loses efficiency and needs major repairs later in its life.

Premises in factory costs

The economical use of building space may make a considerable difference to the company's total profitability. If different kinds of production or different processes are going on in one large building, its costs may be allocated at £x per square foot. In this case, care is needed that the entire expense is taken with none being overlooked because it relates to dead space such as entrance lobbies and corridors. The following will serve as an example:

Production areas	ft²		£
Process A	5 000	$\frac{5}{15}$ x 30 000 =	10 000
Process B	8 000	$\frac{8}{15}$ x 30 000 =	16 000
Process C	2 000	$\frac{2}{15}$ x 30 000 =	4 000
	15 000	Total cost	30 000
'Dead space'	5 000		
Total area	20 000		

Figure 1:7 illustrates the form recommended for itemising the costs of factory premises. Electricity or other fuel used for heating and lighting the factory should not be duplicated with the fuel used for processing which may have been entered among the direct factory costs.

Building maintenance may tend to be erratic with a very heavy incidence every fourth or fifth year. It may be useful to spread this evenly by making a building maintenance reserve to be treated as an additional expense in the years when little actual maintenance or decoration is carried out. The following will serve as an example:

ACTUAL MAINTENANCE	RESERVE		TOTAL IN THE ACCOUNTS
£	£		£
Year 1	10	20	=	30
Year 2	10	20	=	30
Year 3	10	20	=	30
Year 4	80	−50	=	30
	110	10		120

The figure for factory general expenses would closely resemble the one for factory premises. It would include factory telephone, factory office expenses (time cards, record sheets, etc.,) and all other expenses of the factory not already dealt with in one of the previous figures.

Stock of finished goods

Figure 1:8 shows the accounting form for stock of finished goods. The variation between actual and budget will be caused entirely by quantity and not value per unit. The sales director will have to judge whether any new low level of stock shown is satisfactory or whether efforts will need to be made to bring it back to normal the following month.

Any increase in quantity and value during the month will mean that these figures must be added to the cost of goods sold shown in the trading account.

Monthly Trading Accounts

The trading account is designed to show the straight difference between income from sales and the cost of the goods sold, with a suitable adjustment for the change in value of the stock of finished goods. The result is the gross profit which is then subject to the other overhead expenses which appear in the profit and loss account. This makes it possible to isolate changes in results arising from new terms of trading from changes caused by altering factory costs, from changes in administrative overheads or from different selling expenses.

Some of the facts revealed by these accounts are likely to have special significance for the accountant who is experienced in their interpretation. He should be encouraged to add suitable comments so that he shares the benefit of his knowledge with the departmental managers and directors who may not be so well accustomed to spotting the important points.

Figure 1:9 shows an example of a master sheet for the trading account. The purpose of the trading account is to isolate the sales of manufactured goods from the costs and problems of carrying out the manufacture. This is the sphere of the sales director and his staff, whereas the manufacturing account made a spotlight for the production director. The gross profit represents the straight difference between the sales and the cost of the goods which have been sold. There is no complication with overhead expenses which have been kept strictly to the later stage of the accounts – profit and loss accounts. When results fail to match budgets it is then possible to isolate the trouble instead of having to search through all the records. (See Figure 1:1.)

Adverse variances in the gross profit as a percentage of sales should be investigated. Some of the causes may be:

1   Increases in selling prices not keeping pace with increases in cost or purchase prices
2   A change in the mix of products sold; a larger proportion of those lines which show a lower profit
3   Inaccurate stock taking
4   Stock leakage and pilferage

The following list will suggest other reasons for gross profit deficiencies. Management would need to consider each of these until it arrived at the correct interpretation of why the gross profit was not as budgeted. In certain cases variations in profit could be traced back to prime costs, e.g. labour or fuel costs.

Sales

1   Selling prices lower than planned – accidental or deliberate reductions
2   Discounts to customers have been out of line
3   Failure to invoice goods dispatched

Stock of finished goods

1   The closing stock has been incorrectly counted or identified or priced
2   Value has dropped by a known amount because the goods have deteriorated or gone out of fashion

3   The opening stock was undervalued and has been sold well above the figure shown in the accounts — or vice versa

4   Customers have been given credit for goods returned, but the goods did not arrive

Goods inwards

1   There is a known difference between the actual and forecast cost of goods from own factory or from outside sources

2   Goods booked in and paid for were not received, or were of a lower quality than shown in the records

3   Goods were ordered at one price, which was used for fixing their selling prices, but were invoiced by the suppliers at higher prices (see Chapter 10)

4   Carriage on goods purchased was omitted

Obviously, companies such as retailers and wholesalers, which carry out no manufacturing, will have no manufacturing account. They will start their monthly accounts with a trading account similar to that shown in Figure 1:9 but with no entry for goods from own factory.

Like all ratios, gross profit is not in itself significant as an absolute figure. Where it is of use is as a comparison with what was expected or what was achieved last time, or what other companies might achieve.

Sales in the trading account

The sales in the trading account, shown in Figure 1:10, is intended to highlight the most important points, leaving the more detailed analysis of sales to the sales director and his assistants.

The division of the customers into groups depends on the nature of the trade. It might, for example, be by geographic areas or by the rate of trade discount to which they are entitled. Chapter 6 describes more detailed analyses of sales.

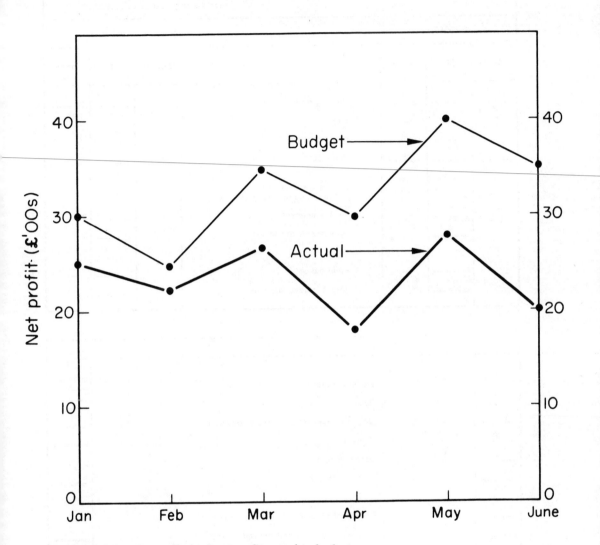

Figure 1:1   Comparison of net profit actual to budget

	BUDGET				ACTUAL	
			Month ending _____			
Quantity	£	% of prime cost		Quantity	£	% of prime cost
	———	———	Raw material		———	———
	———	———	Direct wages		———	———
	———	———	Direct expenses		———	———
═══	═══	═══	Prime cost	═══	═══	═══
	———		Factory costs as listed in part (*b*)		———	
	———		Work in progress		———	
	═══		Total manufacturing costs		═══	
	———		Profit margins		———	
	═══		Total to trading accounts		═══	

(*a*)

£	FACTORY COSTS	£
———	Wages—indirect	———
———	Salaries	———
———	Machinery—upkeep and running depreciation	———
———	Premises	———
———	General expenses	———
═══	Total factory costs	═══
———	Prime cost per unit	———
═══	Total manufacturing cost per unit	═══

(*b*)

Figure 1:2   Master sheet for the manufacturing account

BUDGET				ACTUAL	
Quantity	£	Summarised by departments		Quantity	£
_____	_____	Department 1		_____	_____
_____	_____	Department 2		_____	_____
_____	_____	Department 3		_____	_____
	========	Total			========
Quantity		Summarised by processes		Quantity	£
_____	_____	Process *X*		_____	_____
_____	_____	Process *Y*		_____	_____
_____	_____	Process *Z*		_____	_____
	========	Total			========
£ total	Quantity of finished product	£ per unit	Analysed in proportion to finished materials produced	£ total	Quantity of finished product	£ per unit
_____	_____	_____	Material *A*	_____	_____	_____
_____	_____	_____	Material *B*	_____	_____	_____
_____	_____	_____	Material *C*	_____	_____	_____
========	========	========	Total	========	========	========

Figure 1:3   Direct wages and raw material in manufacturing account

BUDGET					ACTUAL			
				At start of month				
Department			Total		Department			Total
1	2	3			1	2	3	
———	———	———	———	Material	———	———	———	———
———	———	———	———	Direct wages	———	———	———	———
═══	═══	═══	═══		═══	═══	═══	═══
				At end of month				
———	———	———	———	Material	———	———	———	———
———	———	———	———	Direct wages	———	———	———	———
═══	═══	═══	═══		═══	═══	═══	═══
———	———	———	———	Change	———	———	———	———
Repeat for quantities								

Figure 1:4   Work in progress account

BUDGET				ACTUAL		
Quantity	£	Average hourly rate		Quantity	£	Average hourly rate
———	———	———	Maintenance engineers	———	———	———
———	———	———	Cleaners	———	———	———
———	———	———	Security officers	———	———	———
———	———	———	Foreman, etc	———	———	———
———	———	———	etc	———	———	———
═══	═══	═══	Total	═══	═══	═══

Figure 1:5   Account of indirect wages in factory costs

BUDGET					ACTUAL			
Department			Total		Department			Total
1	2	3			1	2	3	
				Running and upkeep costs				
				Fuel – oil gas etc				
				Spares				
				Depreciation				
				(*a*) On original cost of machines				
				(*b*) Provision for higher replacement cost due to inflation				
				Total				

Figure 1:6   Machinery in factory cost account

BUDGET					ACTUAL			
Department			Total		Department			Total
1	2	3			1	2	3	
				Rent				
				Rates				
				Electricity				
				Building maintenance				
				Insurance, etc				
				Total				

Figure 1:7   Premises in factory cost account

At start of month								
	Quantity	Value				Quantity	Value	
		Each	Total				Each	Total
Material A	_____	£_____	_____		Material A	_____	£_____	_____
Material B	_____	_____	_____		Material B	_____	_____	_____
Material C	_____	_____	_____		Material C	_____	_____	_____

At end of month								
	BUDGET					ACTUAL		
	Quantity	Value				Quantity	Value	
		Each	Total				Each	Total
Material A	_____	£_____	_____		Material A	_____	£_____	_____
Material B	_____	_____	_____		Material B	_____	_____	_____
Material C	_____	_____	_____		Material C	_____	_____	_____

Change during the month				
	BUDGET		ACTUAL	
Change	Quantity	£	Quantity	£
Material C	_____	_____	_____	_____

Figure 1:8   Stock of finished goods record

BUDGET			ACTUAL	
Quantity	£		Quantity	£
————	————	Goods from own factory (transfer from manufacturing account)	————	————
————	————	Goods bought from other makers	————	————
═══	═══	Total	═══	═══
+————	+————	Change in stock of finished goods	+————	+————
————	————	Cost of goods sold	————	————
————	————	Sales	————	————
	═══	Gross profit		═══
	————%	Gross profit as a percentage of sales		————%

Month ending ————————

Figure 1:9 Master sheet for the trading account

	Material		Total £		Material		Total £
				Values Date _____			
	BUDGET				**ACTUAL**		
A	B	C			A	B	C	
£___ ___ ___			___	To group *S* customers	£___ ___ ___			___
___ ___ ___			___	To group *T* customers	___ ___ ___			___
___ ___ ___			___	To group *V* customers	___ ___ ___			___
═══ ═══ ═══			═══	Total	═══ ═══ ═══			═══

Repeat for quantity

Figure 1:10   Sales in the trading account

2

Monthly Profit and Loss Account and Balance Sheet

Monthly Profit and Loss Account

The object of the profit and loss account is to show the effect of the different kinds of overhead expenses and to arrive at the final net profit for the period. In most companies these overheads are a serious drain on total income and they deserve careful attention.

Figure 2:1 shows an example of a profit and loss account. Other subsections of the profit and loss account may be relevant to particular types of trade. Each company needs to modify this general pattern to suit its own circumstances.

Accounting ratios

Net profit as a percentage of sales is a key ratio. Any variation of gross profit percentage between budget and actual will be directly reflected in the same variation between the budget and the actual results in the net profit. Therefore gross profit differences should be noted before starting to look for other reasons for variances in the net profit. For example:

	FORECAST	ACTUAL	DIFFERENCE
Gross profit	50%	48.8%	1.2%
Net profit	10%	8.8%	1.2%

Actual expenses must be identical with the budget as a percentage of sales because the entire variation is accounted for in the gross profit margin.

On the basis that (a) some expenses would be expected to vary according to the volume of sales and (b) expenses would rarely vary according to gross profit margins, a more satisfactory approach to ratios may be to take each type of expenses as a percentage of sales and look at variations on their own merits and not as a relationship to net profit. Figure 2:2 illustrates the format recommended.

Expenses

Many of the overhead expenses arise on a half-yearly or annual basis. For these r.1onthly accounts it is important to take into reckoning the correct proportion of the latest level of these items and not some out-of-date historical level.

A cross-check is needed at least once a year to make sure that every kind of spending is finding its way into the monthly accounts. Any item which is not already included in the manufacturing or trading account must come into the profit and loss account. Wherever possible the headings for each type of expense in the profit and loss account should relate to the responsibilities of one executive. For example, the sales director might be held responsible for all sales expenses as well as for achieving sales. It is relatively easy to sell goods if the costs incurred are ignored. On the other hand, the company secretary or accountant might be responsible for the administration costs.

Figure 2:3 shows a division of expenses with administration, directors and finance charges divided in proportion to the respective levels of gross profit. However, a more accurate division may be possible. For example, finance charges may be related to the value of assets tied up in the factory and in the trading activity respectively.

Figures 2:4 to 2:6 show the breakdown of expenses according to department for distribution, sales and administration. The numerous supplementary expenses of employing staff should be entered under each type of expense, with the salaries of the employees to whom they relate. Sales staff extras, for example, would be in the sales expenses. These extras include employer's national insurance, superannuation contributions, welfare arrangements, etc.

List of directors' remuneration

A list of directors' remuneration, including salaries, superannuation contributions and other extras, should be kept separately. This sheet, shown in Figure 2:7, should be kept strictly confidential. Basic salaries should be distinguished from the bonus payments which can be considered a true expense in arriving at a profit, and should be included in the profit and loss account.

Exceptional payments, such as compensation for loss of office, should be entered below the supplementary list with a brief explanation. To introduce them into the profit and loss account would be to confuse the contrast of normal expenses and profit.

Balance Sheets

In many companies the preparation of the balance sheet is skipped from the monthly accounts and is only used for the annual published accounts. This saves a little time, but it leaves the other accounts open to some doubt because a balance sheet would prove they were basically correct, although not necessarily correct in detail. The balance sheet will not balance if the double-entry book-keeping leading up to the trading and profit and loss accounts has not been completed accurately.

A comparison of balance sheets at the start and finish of a period will show the overall profit made during the period, although without any of the detail which would show how this has been created. The formula is 'opening balance of shareholders' funds minus closing balance of shareholders' funds; plus dividend declared during the period; less new issues of shares for cash (as distinct from bonus issues)'. The result equals the net profit for the period after tax.

The balance sheet will be for restricted circulation to the directors and accountant and not to the departmental managers. It shows the changes in assets and gives a useful overall picture. However, for management purposes the statement of sources and application of funds is more instructive and is likely to be used in preference to the balance sheet in the search for information about changes in assets and liabilities. This is described in Chapter 4.

Figure 2:8 shows the format of a typical balance sheet giving the total funds invested in the business at one moment in time. The significance of the various kinds of assets is discussed fully in Chapters 3 and 4.

In some companies a bank overdraft is treated as a current liability on the grounds that legally it is repayable at very short notice. Although this is strictly correct and some banks do press their clients with impossible demands during times of credit squeeze, the reality for many firms is that the overdraft is a continuing liability. It is constantly renewed and so is as much part of the permanent capital as the long-term loans and share capital, except that it varies daily in amount.

Patents are wasting assets with a limited life span. They must be written off over their legal life, or earning life, and each month the amount written off will appear as one of the overhead expenses in the profit and loss account.

Goodwill is different because it increases rather than reduces in value when the trade is being exploited successfully. There are some who believe that it should therefore remain as an asset at cost and not be written off against profits unless the trade is depleted. Others, however, believe that, as goodwill only arises where a business had been acquired for more than the net asset value, it should not be written up when profits increase.

Trade investments normally remain in the balance sheet at cost unless there is a significant and permanent change in their value. In this case a sharp fall would be entered separately as an exceptional loss at the foot of the profit and loss account. Alternatively a sharp rise would be matched by an addition to capital reserves on the balance sheet but with no entry on the profit and loss account. Only when investments are actually sold and a positive profit is realised would they cause an exceptional profit to appear at the foot of the profit and loss account.

Some companies declare dividends twice a year. In the monthly accounts the next anticipated dividend may be regarded as a current liability. It should not be ignored merely because the directors have not as yet made a positive decision to recommend it. A forecast of their recommendation should be made even though they will not consider it binding when the time comes.

Cumulative Total of Monthly Accounts

Although each month must stand on its own, it is also useful to see the cumulative total building up to the whole financial year. For this it is adequate to take only key figures. Figure 2:9 shows a cumulative summary.

The reserves are entered next to the ordinary share capital to stress the fact that they do indeed belong to these shareholders. The ordinary shareholders have increased their original investment by the amount of the reserves which represent past profits retained within the company. A common mistake is to see the reserves as belonging to the company.

With a few exceptions, where hybrid rights have been created, preference shareholders have no part in the reserves; their agreed fixed dividend having been paid, they have no further rights against the company, so long as it is solvent and a going concern.

Summary of tax liabilities

Corporation tax.   For companies formed since 5 April 1965 and for older companies which have changed their accounting date, this tax is payable nine months after the end of the financial year. For older established companies which have not changed their accounting date, the tax is payable on 1 January in the tax year following the tax year in which their annual accounts have ended.

Value added tax.   Unless a significant proportion of a company's turnover is represented by zero-rated or exempt supplies, and assuming that sales exceed purchases, the company acts as tax collector and the difference between the total output tax (VAT charged to customers) and input tax (VAT charged by suppliers) is payable quarterly to Customs and Excise.

Tax deducted from annual interest.   A limited company paying out debenture interest or other kinds of annual interest will deduct income tax at the standard rate. The gross figure is the true cost to appear in the profit and loss account.

Advance corporation tax.   A limited company paying out dividends has a liability for the tax imputed to shareholders at the standard rate (currently 30 per cent). A dividend of £70 000 will therefore attract advance corporation tax of £30 000, which would be set off against the company's mainstream corporation tax liability.

Tax deducted from earnings.   The tax deducted from salaries and wages by the PAYE system is payable to the collector of taxes monthly on the nineteenth day of the month. The true cost of wages and salaries to the company is this gross amount, which should appear in the monthly accounts and costing system. In the cash flow (Chapter 3) the new wages/salaries appear as they become payable but the PAYE is shown on the nineteenth of the month.

Both employers' and employees' National Insurance contributions are due at the same time as PAYE and will be included in the same cheque to the collector of taxes.

Corporation Tax

Although the calculation of corporation tax is made only once a year, the tax payable is of considerable interest to directors and it should be kept in mind when preparing monthly accounts. Monthly accounts will be scrutinised for expenses allowable or not allowable for tax purposes and how capital allowances will affect taxable profit.

Corporation tax is payable at an interval of between nine and twenty-one months after the end of the financial year depending on the company. If the interval is between nine and twelve months there will only be one liability outstanding at any time and it is sufficiently close to be described as a current liability. When the interval is more than twelve months two lots of corporation tax will appear in each annual balance sheet:

1   For the profit of the year before the one which has just ended. This will become a current liability because the date for settlement is now quite near
2   For the profit of the year which has just ended. This will be placed amongst the long-term liabilities (next below the long-term loans) because it is not due for more than a year

Figure 2:10 illustrates the method for analysing the results of profit after corporation tax.

A standard form of adjustment of trading profit for corporation tax purposes is shown in Figure 2:11. The capital allowances are dealt with in more detail in Chapter 9. Occasional capital gains from a profitable disposal of land, buildings or of goodwill is discussed in Chapter 9.

Tax losses

When an outright loss for an accounting period is calculated for corporation tax purposes, there is a choice of ways of obtaining tax relief. The normal method which operates almost automatically is to carry forward the loss to the future and set it against future profits for the same trade. This has two drawbacks from the company's point of view:

1   There is a delay before the tax relief is effective
2   Tax relief may never be obtained at all if the trade fails to regain a profit-making basis. It is not possible to set the loss against future profits from a different trading activity carried on by the same company, so a change in the nature of the business to restore profitability will not secure tax relief

The alternative method applying at the taxpayer's request is for the loss to be set against all sources of income (trading profit and non-trading income such as from investments) for the immediately preceding accounting year. This has the double advantage of:

1   Giving tax relief promptly with a refund of any tax which has already been paid for that preceding year
2   Being possible to set the loss against investment income or estate income if the previous year's trading profit is inadequate to offset the loss completely

This matter concerns the management because they must be aware of the benefits of instructing the auditors to complete the loss-making annual accounts with a minimum of delay and putting forward the claim for tax relief at the earliest possible date. The occasion of having made a loss is likely to be a time at which the benefit to the cash flow through the tax relief is of special value.

Budget		Month ending _____	Actual
	Distribution expenses		
	Sales expenses		
	Administration expenses		
	Directors' remuneration		
	Finance charges		
	Total overheads		
	Gross profit		
	Net trading profit		
	Factory profit from manufacturing account		
	Total profit		

Figure 2:1   Profit and loss account

BUDGET				ACTUAL	
£	%			£	%
		Sales			
		Distribution expenses			
		Sales			
		Administration			
		Directors			
		Finance			
		Total overheads			
		Net profit			
		Gross profit			

Figure 2:2   Accounting ratios

BUDGET				ACTUAL		
Trading	Manufacturing	Total		Trading	Manufacturing	Total
———		———	Distribution	———		———
———		———	Sales	———		———
═══				═══		
———	———	———	Administration	———	———	———
———	———	———	Directors	———	———	———
———	———	———	Finance	———	———	———
═══	═══	═══		═══	═══	═══
———	———	———	Gross profit	———	———	———
═══	═══	═══	Net profit	═══	═══	═══

Figure 2:3   **Division of expenses**

BUDGET £			ACTUAL £
		Month ending ———————	
	Dispatch warehouse		
———	Fixed—	Salaries	———
———		Premises	———
———		Plant and equipment depreciation	———
———	Variables—	Wages	———
———		Plant and equipment running costs	———
	Motor lorries and vans		
———	Fixed—	Drivers' wages	———
———		Managers' salary	———
———		Vehicle depreciation	———
———		Insurance	———
———		Licences	———
———	Variables—	Fuel oil	———
———		Repairs	———
═══	Total		═══

Figure 2:4   **Distribution expenses**

BUDGET £		ACTUAL £
	Month ending _____	
_____	Salaries — Manager	_____
_____	Representatives	_____
_____	Representatives commissions	_____
_____	Representatives expenses	_____
_____	Market research	_____
_____	Advertising	_____
_____	Sales office and showroom premises	_____
_____	Telephone and postages	_____
_____	Total	_____

Figure 2:5   Sales expenses

BUDGET £		ACTUAL £
	Month ending _____	
_____	Stationery	_____
_____	Office equipment and furniture	_____
	Office premises costs :	
_____	Rent	_____
_____	Rates	_____
_____	Electricity, etc	_____
_____	Insurance	_____
_____	Clerical staff	_____
_____	Legal expenses	_____
_____	Postage	_____
_____	Telephone	_____
_____	Total	_____

Figure 2:6   Administration expenses

BUDGET £		ACTUAL £
	Basic salaries for executive duties:	
————	Managing director	————
————	Mr *P*	————
————	Mr *Q*	————
	Director's fees for strictly directorial duties:	
————	Managing director	————
————	Mr *P*	————
————	Mr *Q*	————
════	Sub–total	════
	Bonus and supplementary payments based on company's profits:	
————	Managing director	————
————	Mr *P*	————
————	Mr *Q*	————
════	Total	════

Figure 2:7   Confidential list of directors' remuneration

			As at _____	

ASSETS

Fixed assets: Freehold land and buildings (at valuation 1971) _____

Leasehold factory and offices _____

Sub-total _____

	At cost	Depreciation	
Plant and machinery	_____	_____	_____
Motor vehicles	_____	_____	_____
Office and showroom fixtures	_____	_____	_____

Sub-total _____

Intangible assets: Goodwill, patents, trademarks _____

Trade investments _____

Total fixed assets _____

Current assets: Raw material, work in progress _____

Trading stock _____

Finished goods _____

Sub-total _____

Trade debtors _____

Cash in hand _____

Tax reserve certificates _____

Total current assets _____

Less current liabilities : Trade creditors _____

Corporation tax _____

Proposed dividend _____ _____ _____

Overall total _____

LIABILITIES

Share capital: Ordinary shares _____

Reserves _____

Total of ordinary shareholders' funds _____

Preference shares at _____ % _____

Total of all shareholders' funds _____

Long-term loans at _____ % _____

Bank overdraft _____

Overall total _____

Figure 2:8   Balance sheet

	Period _____
	In financial year from _____

BUDGET		ACTUAL
_____	Prime cost	_____
_____	Factory overheads	_____
_____	Total	_____
_____	Addition for factory profit	_____
_____	Costs transferred to trading account	_____
_____	Completed goods purchased from other manufactures	_____
_____	Increase in stock of finished goods	_____
_____	Cost of goods sold	_____
_____	Sales	_____
_____	Gross profit on trading	_____
_____	Gross profit on manufacture	_____
_____	Total gross profit	_____
_____	Overhead expenses	_____
_____	Net trading profit	_____

Figure 2:9   Manufacturing, trading and profit and loss account cumulative summary

FORECAST		ACTUAL
£_____	Profit before corporation tax, I month	£_____
_____%	Return on total funds of_____	_____%
x 12 for annual rate		x 12 for annual rate
£_____	Profit after corporation tax	£_____
_____%		_____%
x 12		x 12
_____%		_____%

Figure 2:10   Analysis of results before and after corporation tax

Net profit   _____

  Legal expenses   _____

  Loss on sale of machine   _____

  Depreciation   _____

  Entertainment of customers   _____

  General reserve for bad debts   _____   _____

  Total   _____

  Investment income   _____

  Interest on tax reserve certificates   _____

  Capital allowances, subject of a separate calculation _____

  Balance liable to tax   _____

  Total   _____

Figure 2:11   Adjustment of the net profit for corporation tax purposes

3

Short-Term Cash Budget

Short-term cash budgets are necessary to make sure that the bank balance remains satisfactory at all times. Four months is a fair time for a short-term budget. Beyond four months the long-term budget takes over because there is time to:

1   Change funds from non-liquid to liquid form
2   Introduce additional funds
3   Modify plans so that fewer funds will be needed

In the shorter period of less than three months there is little chance to carry out the adjustments mentioned above, except as serious panic measures which may be harmful to the business. There is little scope for modifying the bank balance over a short period by withholding some payments beyond their due dates. The company which makes a regular practice of delaying payments until the latest possible date will have used up all this elasticity. Furthermore, it may discover itself penalised as suppliers grow weary of waiting for their money. If deliveries of urgently needed materials or the servicing of machinery are delayed by disgruntled suppliers the company's own output and profit may be badly hit.

Conversely, where supplies of funds are found to be plentiful, either temporarily or for a long period, there is scope for management skill in making extra profits. Buying terms for raw materials, for example, are often favourable for the company which can offer payment by return of post, because either the supply price will be reduced or a discount for prompt cash settlement will be agreed.

Cash Flow Budget

The cash flow budget should be broken down into weeks so that the balance can be examined for each separate week rather than at the end of the month. The reason for this is that, although the balance at the end of the month may be the same as at the beginning, there may have been considerable variations within the month and urgent action may have to be taken to delay some outgoings or to obtain payments ahead of normal settlement dates. Figure 3:1 illustrates the form which can be used for this purpose.

This budget should be prepared at least once a month and suitable extracts should be made from the cash forecast. Although the purchasing officer will not normally be included in the inner cabinet of executives who are fully aware of the company's bank balance, he should be given instructions each month. Where the trade is seasonal or the liquid funds position is variable for some other reason, his instructions may well vary from one period to another. He should certainly be told whether to seek longest possible settlement terms or to offer prompt payment in return for concessions.

Cash Receivable Budget

The income included in the cash flow budget (Figure 3:1) is obtained from the forecast of cash receivable illustrated in Figure 3:2. The cash receivable budget is not the place for optimism but a realistic appraisal of what is likely to happen.

The figure for credit sales in each week should represent the amounts the customers are expected to pay. For example, standard terms may show that all December sales will be paid for during the week ending 3 February, whereas experience shows that it is unlikely that all money due will be received by that date.

The cash forecast must pick up not only routine incomings from customers but also longer interval items and exceptional items. The man responsible for applications for VAT refunds and government grant claims should have some approximate idea when they will arrive.

Whilst it is seldom that there will be income from the sale of fixed assets, this item should be included on the record so that it is not overlooked. Moreover, the net income from investments after deduction of income tax appears on this budget although the gross figure is the true income to be entered in the profit and loss account.

Cash Payable Budget

The outgoings included in the cash flow budget (Figure 3:1) are taken from a budget of cash payable shown in Figure 3:3. This budget is normally much larger and more complex than the list of cash receivable. This budget includes:

Wages and salaries, including	Superannuation contributions
all bonus, overtime	Electricity, gas, rent, etc.
and commission entries	Rates
PAYE and National Insurance	Dividends
Expenses	Interest payments
Purchases	Directors' fees

Some items, such as insurance premiums, gas and electricity, are payable at long intervals, annually, half-yearly or quarterly — or monthly in some instances. All of these must be foreseen and included in the cash forecast. If their amount is not known exactly a guess is much better than to ignore them entirely.

Depreciation

Depreciation is a true expense in the manufacturing account, or profit and loss account, but it has no place in the cash flow budget. This is a frequent cause of misunderstanding because it is not at first clear how the cash flow can be made to tie up with the profit and loss and manufacturing accounts if the depreciation is left out of one and included in the other.

The fact is that incoming cash equals profit plus depreciation plus all other costs. All other costs are also part of the outgoing cash, except for one or two minor adjustments relating to outstanding balances at the start and finish of a period. Therefore, net incoming cash is equal to total cash from sales. For example, 100, less outgoing cash to meet expenses 70, leaving net incoming cash 30, which equals profit plus depreciation.

Remedial procedures

The accountant responsible for preparation of the cash budget should inform the appropriate executives when the anticipated balance is unsatisfactory. The executives should take the necessary action, unless the accountant is filling more than one role, for he will not normally carry out the action himself nor issue instructions but he may well offer advice. The actions which might be taken, listed below, call for management skill to foresee their side effects.

Forecast shows a temporarily excessive overdraft

1   Delay making some payments. Great care is needed not to antagonise suppliers or incur penalties
2   Delay making some purchases and plan to live off stocks for a short period
3   Press some customers to make their payments more promptly

Forecast shows the overdraft repeatedly above the agreed level (see Chapter 4)

1   Negotiate a larger overdraft agreement with the bank manager
2   Make a permanent reduction in stocks — this may be dangerous and may lead to loss of efficiency
3   Make a permanent reduction in credit allowed to customers. This is often extremely difficult
4   Factor the trade debts
5   Persuade suppliers to wait longer for settlement
6   Reduce the investment in fixed assets (see Chapter 9). This takes time
7   Sell some investments
8   Raise a fresh long-term loan
9   Issue fresh share capital

Forecast shows temporary surplus of funds in the bank current account

1   Make a transfer to a deposit account. Remember to withdraw from the deposit at the right time. Seven days' notice of withdrawal is commonly required
2   Seek some other short-term investment. Remember that it must be possible to withdraw whenever necessary

Forecast shows permanent surplus of funds in the bank current account (see Chapter 4)

1   Repay some long-term loans
2   Expand the business to fresh ventures
3   Declare larger dividends. This is often not a good plan in a company whose main shareholders are already higher rate and investment income surcharge payers
4   Buy some trade investments to strengthen the firm's connection with its suppliers or customers
5   Offer prompt settlement terms to suppliers in return for concessions on prices or cash discounts
6   Offer delayed settlement terms to customers as inducement to place bigger orders. This may be dangerous owing to greater risk of bad debts

Stabilising the cash balance

In most companies the bank balance varies from one month to the next. Spending is spread throughout the month but the income is mostly received at the end of the month, so that the bank balance is lowest at mid-month.

   Graphs, such as those shown in Figure 3:4, will readily reveal the fluctuations in bank balance and enable management to take action to stabilise it at an acceptable level. The benefits of doing this are well demonstrated in the examples which show three companies, *A*, *B* and *C*, all with an identical rise and fall of their bank balance from month to month. In each firm the balance most favourable to the company is 20 000 better than the least favourable balance of that same company.

All three companies have agreed with their bank manager on an overdraft of £25 000. Company *A* starting in January has an overdraft of only £5 000. Only very briefly at two points during the year, mid-April and mid-September, does the overdraft hit the agreed limit. Throughout most of the year there is a comfortable margin of safety between the actual overdraft and the limit.

In company *B* the starting point is an overdraft of £20 000 in January which means it is more heavily dependent on the bank support than *A* to the extent of £15 000. For much of the year the limit of overdraft has been exceeded which puts *B* in a very weak position. Each month the bank manager's patience will wear thinner until it is finally exhausted and he brings the business to an abrupt halt.

For a forecast like this, company *B* should either find some more permanent capital, from one of the sources discussed in Chapter 4, or approach the bank manager for a revised limit.

The danger to *B* is not so much in having a large overdraft as an absolute figure as in having gone beyond the level acceptable to the bank. The point can soon be reached where the bank refuses to honour the cheques. They will bounce back from the suppliers and very quickly there will be a loss of reputation which could jeopardise *B*'s sources of raw materials.

Meanwhile company *C* has started the year with £25 000 better bank balance than *A*. Not only has the overdraft facility not been used at all but for all but an odd two weeks there has been a large faithful balance lying idle in the bank. This company should query whether it is wise to run its bank account in this way or whether more funds could be put to good use in extra business activities or perhaps some short-term investments could be considered.

Period: I January to 31 March									
	January				February				March
Week ending	6	13	20	27	3	10	17	24	2
Bank balance at start of week Add income	— — — — — — — —								
Total Deduct outgoings	═ ═ ═ ═ — — — —								
Balance at the end of the month	═ ═ ═ ═								

Figure 3:1   Cash flow budget — three months

Period: I January to 31 March												
	January				February				March			
Week ending	6	11	20	27	3	10	17	24	2			
From cash sales												
From credit sales												
From VAT refunds and government grants												
From sale of fixed assets												
From new loans and share issues												
From tax refunds												
From investment income: interest dividends												
Total for the week	═	═	═	═	═	═	═	═	═			

Figure 3:2   Budget of cash receivable

Three months — I January to 31 March						
	January				February	March
Week ending	6	13	20	27		
Wages						
Salaries						
PAYE and National Insurance						
Petty cash expenses						
Weekly purchase accounts						
Monthly purchase accounts						

New plant and machinery:
  purchases
  hire purchase						

Superannuation contributions						

Quarterly accounts:
  electricity
  gas
  rent (etc)						

Half-yearly accounts: general rates (etc)						
Annual accounts: insurance premiums (etc)						

Dividends:
  (*a*) amounts to shareholders
  (*b*) Advance Corporation Tax						

Interest payments:
  (*a*) net amounts to lenders
  (*b*) income tax to Revenue						

Directors' fees						
Total						

Figure 3:3   Budget of cash payable

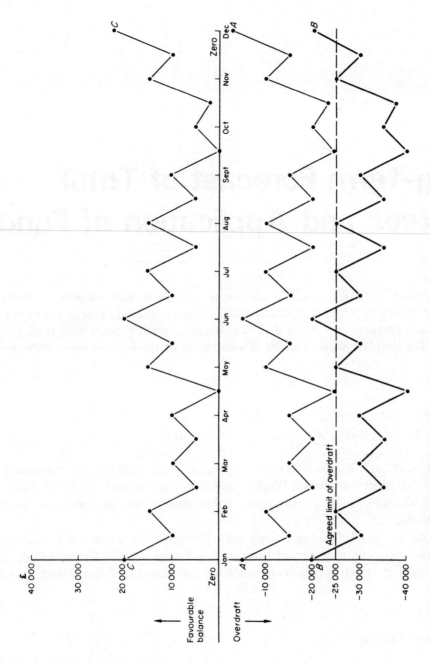

Figure 3:4   Alternative possibilities for bank overdraft

4

Long-Term Forecast of Total Sources and Application of Funds

The long-term forecasts include all kinds of assets and liabilities, unlike the short-term forecasts which essentially revolve around the liquid position of the bank balance. Accountants use many different ways of setting out a long-term forecast. Probably the simplest way is in the familiar form of the balance sheet with columns for:

1   Present figures
2   Figures forecast as at a future date
3   The changes taking place between the two dates

A budget, such as the one illustrated in Figure 4:1, showing the forecast a year ahead is the most common. Where long-term investment in fixed assets and expansion of trade is being considered, there should also be forecasts over much longer periods.

In the early years following a company's formation or when drastic changes are being considered, a shorter period forecast, say for six months ahead, will be useful.

The budget is divided into two sections: application of funds and sources of funds.

Application of Funds

Applications of funds are assets of all kinds including:

1   Land and building
2   Plant and machinery

3   Trading stocks
4   Trade debtors — customers who have not paid their accounts
5   Cash in hand
6   Investments of any kind
7   Goodwill, patents and trademarks

Depreciation of plant and machinery represents a reduction in value. This could be entered as if it were a source of funds but it is more straightforward and easier to understand if it is shown as a reduction in the application of funds.

The long-term forecast may show a gap but this is fictitious as a gap is not really possible. Anything purchased but not paid for creates additional creditors, although they may not be the trade creditors in the normal sense. These creditors are likely to become impatient if their accounts are not settled. So while there is a gap, a way of filling it has to be found or the company has become insolvent.

The directors normally examine the forecast and its supporting notes, item by item, until all possibilities have been considered. It is probable that the gap will be closed by making a lot of small adjustments rather than a single massive change.

The following will give some ideas of the type of changes which could be made:

1   Plant and motor vehicles now to be taken on lease instead of purchase
2   Fewer trade investments to be acquired
3   Smaller trading stocks to be held
4   Tightening of credit terms to customers
5   Issue of new share capital
6   Extra long-term loan to be raised
7   Trade suppliers to be asked to give longer settlement terms

Revised Forecasts

A revised edition of the forecast will show the position after making the directors' changes. It is vital that the necessary action is taken to make sure this really fits the revised rather than the original forecast. For this reason the forecast should be regarded as a tool of management rather than that of the financial director alone. Although the revised forecast will have been made with the help and agreement of the various departmental managers, each one will have seen only those aspects of the forecast which concern his own department.

When the forecast has been brought to a satisfactory balance each executive will need to watch the items within his control and see that they are kept in line with the forecast as the year proceeds. Alternatively, if changes are unavoidable, he will give as much warning as possible to the financial director who will have the responsibility of revising the balance of the sources and applications.

Comparison of the Effect of High and Low Gearing

Inquiries for the terms of new loans by the end of the year should be made at the end of each period. It is dangerous to take borrowing facilities for granted and better terms can be negotiated when the company is not under pressure but can still adjust its requirements if necessary.

Large loans change the proportion of loans to shareholders' funds and this is called the gearing of the capital. The benefits and dangers of higher gearing should be examined, so that on occasion a comparison of the effect of high and low gearing, shown in Figure 4:2, may be needed to provide the necessary information for management to decide whether new loans or additional share capital would be preferable.

It is normally the function of the Board to study these figures with professional advisers. This takes time, and, for this reason, forecasts are made well into the future, at the very least four months, to allow enough time for action such as obtaining a new issue of shares.

Other executives may be involved in having to produce an accurate forecast of profit as a return on capital employed, particularly in its relationship to new assets which are to be purchased with the proceeds of the loans. The other executives may also be required to produce their forecasts of income and expenditure which show how much borrowing is going to be necessary.

Summary of Trading Stocks

As one of the main reasons for applications of funds being increased, and probably the most fruitful source of savings, trading stocks should be shown on a separate summary, such as the one illustrated in Figure 4:3. There should, however, be a minimum level of stock necessary. Discussions with numerous executives will be needed to avoid demanding stock reductions which could only lead to inefficiency. To fall below the optimum level may be as harmful to the business as to hold excessive quantities. Perhaps more so.

Summary of Trade Debtors

Figure 4:4 shows a summary of trade debtors with columns for change and revised plan. A subdivision into types of goods being sold would only be useful if there were substantial differences between them. For example, if material *C*, shown in the example, were a new product, quite different from *A* and *B* for which new markets are being sought, the development of *C* would be properly treated on its own merits.

The subject of trade debtors is discussed further in Chapter 6.

Sources of Funds

Sources of funds are liabilities of all kinds including:

1 Share capital
2 Reserves, including retained profits
3 Long, medium and short-term loans
4 Corporation tax
5 Proposed dividends
6 Trade creditors (suppliers waiting for payment)

Where a surplus of cash is temporary — for example, where it will be needed to pay for major installations of plant or a new factory — a brief note to this effect should be added.

The primary concern of the directors, particularly the managing director, will be the net change. Where there is to be little change there are likely to be few problems unless repayment of loans or redeemable share capital is going to fall due.

The methods by which companies may raise additional funds are:

1 A bank loan or overdraft from a joint stock banking company. The 1981 Budget introduced the Pilot Loan Scheme, with the Government guaranteeing 80 per cent of a loan not exceeding £75 000 repayable within seven to ten years, restricting the bank's risk to 20 per cent.
2 Merchant banks. These differ slightly from the joint stock banking companies in that they are often more willing to supply additional capital for private companies and/or the acquisition of shares from a major shareholder.
3(*a*) Bills of exchange and acceptance credits. These are used particularly for export sales and they enable the company to receive payment by discounting the bill of exchange at its own bank while the customer has not yet paid his account.

(*b*) ECGD The Export Credit Guarantees Department is not in itself a direct source of additional funds but it does supply excellent backing by which exporters may obtain bank funds at reasonable rates.
4 Industrial hire purchase of plant and machinery and other equipment. The director of the Finance Houses Association Limited, 14 Queen Anne's Gate, London SW1, will supply details of these facilities, which are available from a wide range of industrial finance companies.
5 The leasing of equipment. It is now possible to obtain leasing facilities for almost all kinds of machinery and plant and motor vehicles and equipment generally. In some instances the manufacturers of the assets will themselves arrange the lease facilities and in other cases they will introduce the purchaser to finance companies.
6 Government help in development areas. Although the investment grants on plant and machinery have now been discontinued, government assistance is still available towards companies which wish to set up factory premises in development areas.

These include either grants towards the cost of buildings or premises available on reasonable rents.

7   Assistance by local authorities and by new town development corporations. The local authorities have power to make loans to individuals or to corporate bodies for the erection of buildings on land which an authority has sold or let for this purpose.

8   IFCL. The Industrial and Finance Corporation Limited of 91, Waterloo Road, London SE1 is a major source of funds for small and medium-sized industrial companies. They advertise amounts from £5000 to £2 million available for expansion, management buyouts, or starting a new business from scratch, either in long-term loans or equity capital.

9   EDITH. The Estate Duties Investment Trust Limited bears a close resemblance to IFCL and is based at the same address. They concentrate particularly on providing funds where there is either an immediate or anticipated future need by the leading owners of private companies for capital transfer tax to be met. Capital transfer tax was introduced by the 1975 Finance Act, which abolished estate duty.

10   Insurance companies. Insurance companies will often advance funds on a long-term basis against the security of land and buildings. They are not usually particularly interested in supplying companies with working capital.

11   Capital issues. Private limited companies of a suitable size may issue shares to the general public by means of a stock exchange quotation. This is a specialist topic to be regarded as a once for all long-term possibility. As a rough guide, it may be said that the total assets of the company would need to be at least £500 000, while the prospect of annual profits should be not less than £50 000 a year, with a past record of improving profits and the prospect that future profits will advance beyond the opening level.

The Unlisted Securities Market was created in 1980 and its entry requirements are less onerous than those for listing, making it worthy of consideration by small companies. There is no minimum size of issue and the proportion of share capital placed is in the region of 10 per cent.

12   Sale and lease back. Companies which own freehold premises may sell these to financial organisations and lease them back again. Numerous insurance companies, property investment companies and pension funds advertise regularly their willingness to carry out this kind of transaction.

13   The sale of book debts – factoring. This transaction has become steadily more popular. Several companies offer these facilities and it is usual to obtain an introduction to them through the company's normal bankers.

Emergency Expedients

The company may have mapped out its forecast of funds with reasonable care and yet meet with some unexpected crisis which would push the bank overdraft well beyond the agreed limit.

A careful check is needed to make sure that the company is not technically insolvent — unable to meet its obligations. If that were the case there would be no legal option but to go into liquidation.

However, if the directors are satisfied that the emergency is only temporary, and given a little time they will be able to either obtain fresh funds or release funds from tied assets to liquid form, they will look for ways of covering the immediate future.

The following ideas should be used only in the last resort and not regarded as regular ways of meeting a recurring shortage of funds. A company's reputation is easily damaged by making careless use of these emergency measures:

1   Try the bank manager for a temporary extension of the overdraft limit. Offer some personal security, such as a director's own life insurance policy, if really necessary.

2   Ask some customers if they will pay immediately on receipt of goods, or even in advance. This calls for a personal approach at director level and should only be tried with customers of long standing and who are on unusually good terms with the company.

3   Ask some suppliers if they will wait longer than the normal time for payment. Again a personal approach is needed and is more likely to be successful than an impersonal letter. It is dangerous (but not unknown) to keep suppliers waiting without asking their permission.

4   Ask the Collector of Taxes if he will permit a delay in settlement of the corporation tax account. This should not be taken for granted, as the request will only be agreed to if there are exceptional circumstances.

5   Switch from annual to six-monthly basis for renewal of road fund licences. This is a costly method.

6   Switch from annual to monthly payment of insurance premiums. This is moderately costly.

Application of funds

Application of funds	Actual position 31.12.80 £	Budget 31.12.82 £	Change +	Change −
Land and buildings:				
freehold addition				
leasehold				
Plant and machinery:				
written down value				
addition				
—depreciation				
Motor vehicles:				
written down value				
—sale				
purchase				
—depreciation				
Office and showroom fixtures and fittings:				
written down value				
—depreciation				
Goodwill, patents, trademarks:				
—depreciation				
Trade investments:				
investment				
—drops in value				
addition				
Trading stocks				
Trade debtors				
Cash in hand and at bank				
Total				
Net increase overall £				

Sources of funds

Sources of funds	Actual 31.12.80	Forecast 31.12.82	Change +	Change −
Share capital				
Reserves and this year's profit (net after tax and dividend)				
Total shareholders' funds				
Long-term loans				
Bank overdraft				
Corporation tax				
Proposed dividends				
Trade creditors				
(Gap)				
Total				
Net increase overall £				

Figure 4:1   Forecast of sources and application of funds

	High gearing		Low gearing	
Share capital	£ _____	£_____	£_____	£_____
Loan	_____	_____	_____	_____
Total capital	=====	=====	=====	=====
Interest	_%_____	_%_____	_%_____	_%_____
For shareholders (dividends and retained profit)	_%_____	_%_____	_%_____	_%_____
Return on total capital	_%_____	_%_____	_%_____	_%_____

Figure 4:2   Comparison of the effect of high and low gearing

	Original plan	Change		Revised plan
		Detail	Total	
(*a*) Raw materials				
(*b*) Work in progress				
(*c*) Finished goods				
Total	=====	=====	=====	=====

Figure 4:3   Summary of trading stocks

	Original plan	Change	Revised plan
Customers on *standard* credit terms for			
Material *A*			
Material *B*			
Material *C*			
Customers on *extended* credit terms for			
Material *A*			
Material *B*			
Material *C*			
Customers on *prompt* settlement terms for			
Material *A*			
Material *B*			
Material *C*			
Total	=====	=====	=====

Figure 4:4   Summary of trade debtors

5

Records of Production

Management accounting records are not concerned solely with money. Records of production and labour utilisation are an important part of cost accounting and necessary for maintaining a close scrutiny on productivity and efficiency.

These accounting records will not show the cause for a low efficiency rating even when they are maintained weekly, nor will they show how to correct the trouble for the coming week. What they will do is draw attention to low efficiency and the effect it is having on costs. An excess of even 5 pence an hour could make serious inroads into the net profit on a product which is selling against fierce competition.

The fault for low efficiency could be found to lie with any of the following:

1   Poor management and organisation, resulting in delays and operatives waiting for work
2   Supplies of materials from the raw materials warehouse not flowing smoothly into the production department as required
3   Delays caused by machinery breakdowns

Departmental Records

In vast departments, too large for close supervision, there are so many difficulties in sorting out the sources of inefficiency that it may be impossible to trace or eliminate the causes. For this reason, each separate section of the production department will need to produce its own versions of the forms illustrated in this chapter. This might at first seem to be a duplication of clerical work as, in theory, the final output of the completed product should tally with the combined results of all departments. In fact, the separation of production into different sections or smaller departments provides for stronger management control and is much more effective in terms of clerical work involved.

The individual manager, foreman or supervisor for each section should be held personally responsible for keeping the records of his own department, and for making sure they show the true facts to balance up with materials, wages and machine output. Depending on the size of the section, and the nature of the product, he may need some clerical help and this may be supplied by the cost accountant's staff, but this does not shift the responsibility from his own shoulders. It merely gives him the problem of making sure that the work is accurate and kept up to date.

Service departments

All companies have departments or sections which are not directly concerned with production but are nevertheless spending money and making an essential contribution to the profit because the business could not function without them.

Whenever possible some modified version of the daily production records should be prepared for these departments. In a distribution department, for example, the daily dispatch to customers can be the equivalent of daily production. The dispatch of sales invoices can be recorded in the same way with an efficiency rating relating to delay between dispatch of goods and of invoices.

Daily Production Records

In terms of production targets, each day stands alone with its success or failure. What is missed on one day cannot be made good on another day. That other day has its own standards to reach, although extra effort may go some way towards making good a shortage of production, provided excessive costs are not incurred.

This implies a need for daily production records. Figure 5:1 illustrates the format of such a record. The month's total figures are entered in the manufacturing account discussed in Chapter 1. But for a real appreciation of the results management will need to look at the details of the daily figures.

The production manager should decide on his key figures and have them set out clearly, perhaps with the help of a graph. Minor details needed for arriving at the key figures should be kept on supplementary sheets where they may form the basis of discussion between the production manager and departmental managers, foremen, supervisors and others with small area responsibilities. Production figures can, of course, be recorded in terms of shift output on essentially the same documentation.

Figure 5:2 shows an example of a summary of daily production, and Figure 5:3 a summary of efficiency ratings for each day.

A standard unit of measurement is needed to set target levels and to establish comparisons of actual results. A standard unit can be expressed in several ways. The unit used in Figures 5:1 to 5:3 are standard machine hours. This unit is used where machinery is a major expense or is in short supply and the number of machine hours worked each day is important. Quantity of goods produced may be fixed in an exact ratio to machine hours in which case a single statement of quantity will serve the double purpose of proving both production and machine hours.

For example, one machine working for twelve hours gross, with an accepted average loss of two hours for stoppages, gives ten hours net. The operatives, using the machine at an average rate will show ten machine hours of work a day.

Above average efficiency will give an actual output greater than ten machine hours whereas adverse factors will lead to smaller output. Minutes rather than hours may be adopted where a brief 'making' time means minutes are a more suitable unit.

Daily Materials Records

Although the purchase of materials of the correct quantity, quality and price is the task of the purchasing officer, making sure that the materials are used efficiently is the production manager's duty.

Measurement would be by quantity rather than by value because it avoids the complication of price changes. A record of each product is then completed with the raw material used or units produced each day. In other words, the daily records should compare the quantity of production at x units of raw materials per unit of finished goods with the forecast of y units of raw material. For example, one unit of completed material A should take 8 kg of raw material P and 3 kg raw material Q.

Figure 5:4 illustrates the form recommended for recording production efficiency according to material used. The target quantity column for each kind of material is a simple multiplication of the number of units of the finished article produced during the day and the amount of material which should be needed for each unit.

The records should be made up promptly every day and not left till the end of the month, so that any serious discrepancy between material actually used and material needed, according to the costing system, will be noticed without delay.

Although the monthly accounts are primarily concerned with units completed, the daily records should also consider the intermediate stages in production. For example material A in Figure 5:4 as a finished product may have been through three distinct phases in three separate departments. In the first department the work may have been measured by standard hours of labour. Only at the final department is the machine hour the standard unit.

Where the production of material is extremely complex, with a dozen or more different successive processes, it will be necessary to make a dozen or more separate records.

In firms whose production cycle spreads over more than one day there is an awkward complication in building such a chart. If it takes three days for raw material to reach the end of the production line, for example, raw material issued to the department on a Monday should agree with the output of the following Thursday.

It would be a fairly simple matter to adjust the record illustrated in Figure 5:5, so that the actual amount of material is always taken in comparison with that which has been issued from the stores three days earlier. In other words, the source information for the column "actual quantity of *Q*" would be drawn from raw material issues three days prior to the date shown in the date column which relates to the output of the finished product.

Where the time cycle for production is itself erratic, with a variation of work in progress wide enough to distort the daily chart, the weekly quantity of material may require an adjustment for the change in work in progress. One attractive solution is to keep work in progress to an absolute minimum so that its variations are also minimised. However, it is recognised that in some industries work flow cannot be manipulated with this kind of flexibility.

Each separate department should prepare its own daily chart of material used in production. Where the product moves from one department to another, making up successive stages before becoming a completed article ready for sale, the first department will compare the quantity of raw material used with the output at the stage for passing on to department 2. Department 2 in its turn will show in place of raw material the quantity it receives from department 1 of the partially made product, and so on through the subsequent departments until it is completed.

In other words, there is no attempt to make a daily comparison of the final completed product from department 6, say, with the issue of raw material into department 1.

Departmental Labour Summary

Where the chief ingredient of manufacture is the operatives' personal labour, and the machine aspect is negligible, a standard making time may be appropriate. The same comment about gross and net working hours and standard efficiency will apply to this as to machine hours. Efficiency rating is calculated as follows:

$$\frac{\text{Production (standard working hours)}}{\text{Net working hours}} \times 100 = x\%$$

Net working hours equals 10/12 of gross working hours. The difference is the agreed standard allowance of non-productive time for operatives.

Figure 5:5 shows an example of a departmental labour summary using standard labour hours. If there are several different products, the form illustrated in Figure 5:6 is recommended.

Alternatively, production per machine hour may be variable according to the efficiency of the operatives and/or the loading of the machines. In this case a ratio of machine hours, production possible/production achieved, will be needed, giving an efficiency rating for the machine shop. For example:

A machine shop with 40 machines and a target of
    ten hours per machine   400 hours
    Product A 1.5 machine hours per unit 80 units   120 machine hours
    Product B 2.5 machine hours per unit 100 units 250 machine hours
                          Actual total   370
                          Shortage   30
                          Target   400
Hours lost because of strikes/labour shortage/power cuts, etc., Nil

$$\text{Efficiency rating:} \qquad \frac{370}{400} = 92.5 \text{ per cent}$$

Figure 5:7 illustrates an example of a form for recording the actual results in terms of hours with the efficiency rating for each week.

Wage Analysis

It is the production manager's responsibility to make sure that wages paid for labour are satisfactory. This would include both directly productive workers and the indirect workers.

The wages budget for each week is calculated by multiplying the number of standard labour hours by the average rate per standard labour hour. A standard labour hour is the time taken in actual productive work. Each company needs to discover the correct relationship between actual hours and standard hours for its own works.

Figure 5:8 shows the actual results of production in terms of wages.

Separate records should be kept for direct and indirect workers. It would be more satisfactory to balance the wages for directly productive workers daily than weekly if wages records are available. But in many firms the weekly calculation is all that is practical without incurring heavy extra expense in clerical work.

Any adverse difference in the cost per potential standard labour hour and that forecast would be because of either excessive overtime or an above-average proportion of workers on top rates. If the cost per actual standard labour hour is appreciably above the forecast it will probably be a direct result of a low efficiency rating, and management attention should concentrate on the possible reasons for low efficiency.

Date	Completed units of material *A*			Daily target: 400 Standard machine hours				
	Day's total	Cumulative total	Comment	Gross operating hours	Net operating hours	Actual production standard machine hours	Efficiency rating %
May 1	388	388	Short of labour	456	380	388	102%
2	402	790					
3	375	1165					
4							
5							
6							
7							
8							
9							
10							
11							
12							
13							
14							
(etc)							
Total							

Month ending: 31 May

Figure 5:1   Daily production record

Product	Machine hours per unit	Units produced	Total machine hours
A	1.5	80	120
B	2.5	100	250
C	2.3	—	—
D	1.8	—	—
		Total not relevant	370

Figure 5:2   Summary of daily production

Date	Total machine hours available	Hours lost	Net available	Hours of production	Efficiency rating %
1 May	400	Nil	400	370	92.5

Figure 5:3   Summary of efficiency ratings

Completed material *A*   Period: Month ending 31 May

Units of *A* produced	Date	Target quantity of *P*	Actual quantity of *P*	Inefficiency %	Target for *Q*	Actual for *Q*	Inefficiency %
	May 1						
	2						
	3						

Figure 5:4   Daily materials record

Daily target units: ___400___   Period: ___Month ending 31 May___

Standard hours per unit: _0.6_ Total standard hours: _240_

Production units of *A*	Date	Number of operatives	Gross working hours	Net working hours	Production standard labour hours	Efficiency rating %	Day's production	Cumulative
350	May 1	38	264	220	210	95.4	210	210
	2						216	426
	(etc)							

Figure 5:5   Monthly labour summary, showing cumulative daily output

Production units					Date	Number of operatives	Gross working hours	Net working hours	Production standard labour hours	Efficiency rating %	Day's production labour hours	Cumulative labour hours
A	B	C	D	Total								
					May 1							
					2							
					3							
					4							
					5							
					6							
					7							
					(etc)							

Month ending: 31 May

Labour standard hour per completed unit A ————
B ————
C ————
D ————

Figure 5:6   Daily production record for department

Period: month ending 31 May

Week ending	Actual labour hours	Potential standard labour hours	Actual standard labour hours produced	Efficiency rating %
5 May				
12 May				
19 May				
26 May				

Figure 5:7   Summary of actual results in terms of hours

Period: month ending 31 May

Week ending	Actual wages	Add 20% for extras	Total	Potential standard labour hours	Actual standard labour hours produced	Cost per standard labour hours produced	Cost per potential labour hours

Figure 5:8   Summary of actual results in terms of wages

6

Sales Records

Taking orders from customers may coincide with supplying the goods – as in retailing. In this case, records of sales are the same as orders received. On the other hand, the orders may be taken several days or even weeks before the goods are to be delivered. This calls for records of orders taken being kept separately from the records of goods dispatched to customers. To rely on a single record of sales, making it serve a dual purpose, could fail to show that, although dispatch of goods has continued at a satisfactory rate, the supply of new incoming orders has long since dried up.

Figure 6:1 illustrates the stages in making and completing a sale to a customer. The objective of such a timetable is to minimise the number of days between receipt of order and dispatch of goods and to minimise the number of days between dispatch of goods and receipt of cash.

Records of Orders Received

Perhaps the most effective way of meeting objectives is by keeping track of incoming orders. Action stemming from information disclosed by the records of orders received will include:

1   Sales may be stepping ahead of production capacity. Decision and suitable action are needed on one or more of the following steps:

(*a*)   Temporary increase in production by such expedients as overtime working.

(*b*)   Permanent increase in production by double-shift working or by adding to machinery.

(*c*)   Advising customers there will be a longer delay between placing the order and dispatch of goods.

(*d*)   Increasing prices to choke off the excess demand and at the same time to increase profitability. This one must be approached with care.

2 Sales may be lagging behind production capacity. Decision and suitable action are needed on:

(*a*) Promoting more sales by cutting prices or by extra advertising or by engaging extra sales staff. Alternatively a combination of these may be used.

(*b*) Looking for different products and/or new styles or designs or models of the present products.

(*c*) Reducing selling prices to attract more customers. This one needs special care as profit may vanish. The sales director's understanding of profit margins at different levels of output is vital.

(*d*) Reducing production capacity and other facilities to match the low level of sales. This one is difficult where there are heavy overhead costs which cannot readily be cut back.

3 The difference between forecast and actual level of orders received from customers will react on:

(*a*) Raw materials to be purchased.

(*b*) The number of operatives required in the factory and of staff in other departments.

(*c*) The cash flow. Thus the statement of orders received will serve as an early warning system for all other departments.

Sales Orders Fulfilled

In the modern management structure of many companies the dispatch of goods to customers is within the control of the distribution executive (DE). This man will be responsible for the efficiency of:

1   The dispatch warehouse, including:
(*a*)   The physical care of the goods and
(*b*)   The documentation, such as dispatch/advice notes and the initiation of invoices
2   The transport of goods by road, including operating a fleet of lorries or dispatch by hired trucks, rail, sea or air

These problems revolve around getting good results at the most reasonable cost. 'Most reasonable' may not equal 'lowest' because customers' urgent demands may take precedence over strict economy. Difficulties are multiplied when required goods fail to come out of the production department as expected.

In some companies this DE is subject to the sales director's overriding control, whilst in others he meets sales and production executives on equal terms. The closest possible co-operation between sales and distribution departments is essential.

Whatever the pattern of distribution control, the sales director needs prompt and reliable information about goods dispatched to customers. Monthly totals are useful to give an overall picture, but daily statements are equally important. To discover at the end of the month that deliveries have been lagging for three weeks and that certain customers have been let down may be too late to save the company's reputation for reliability.

Management action

1   Where there are ample orders but production steps ahead of dispatch the DE may solve the problem by:
(*a*)   Temporary extra efforts to increase dispatch — for example, by overtime working.
(*b*)   Permanent increase in the warehouse and/or vehicle facilities. Alternatively, or perhaps when the new measures are being worked out, the sales staff will be drawn into the matter. They may decide which customers should be made to wait rather than leave it to chance, or they may contact customers to find which parts of their orders they are most urgently waiting for.
2   Where delays in dispatch are directly the result of factory production lagging behind the forecast, the main remedies lie between sales and production departments. However, until they are brought into line the low dispatch figures will form the basis for action by the sales staff in keeping customers warned about the delays.

The immediate result of sending less goods to customers than had been expected will be to hit the cash flow forecast. Income from debtors next month (or the following month, according to the credit terms) will be low and the bank overdraft will suffer.

Record of Goods Invoiced

Figure 6:2 shows an example of a record of sales invoiced to customers. Preparation of this chart should proceed daily with each day's sales added by closing time of the following day. This means that invoices which are usually a carbon copy of the dispatch notes will have been extended and totalled within twenty-four hours of the goods being sent out. Some types of firms might justify a longer delay and set themselves a target delay of not more than three days, for example, but in general a failure to keep the money up to date is a sign of management weakness. It leads to troubles on:

1   Credit control
2   Preparation of statements
3   Records of sales

Where there are more than four different products it may be better to have several separate sheets rather than to try to cram too many on one page. A sheet for each three or four products, which group naturally together, with their own total plus a sheet for the total of totals would be suitable.

Analysis of Discounts

If the company charges different customers different prices for the same product a very strict control on prices is needed, otherwise it will soon be found that favours are being passed out deliberately or by accident with a corresponding cut in net profit. The effect is identical whether the customers are quoted different basic prices or offered trade discounts. Usually the reason for the variation is that bulk orders justify reductions below standard price. Alternatively, cuts may be made to boost sales in the quiet seasons of the year.

Varying transport costs can also lie behind price differences or variations in revenue from the same product. Control can be achieved in two stages:

1   Where the customers' orders are accepted
2   When the goods are invoiced. The invoicing is under review here

Figure 6:3 shows a form used to analyse discounts to customers. For the purpose of this example it is assumed that the company has set up a scale with basic price and three levels of discounts. A few special customers are quoted individual terms because they buy in tremendous bulk or have great powers of persuasion.

The total daily value of invoices is subdivided accordingly. With a computer it would be quite practicable to do this analysis for each separate product but with mechanical recording it would probably be uneconomic to do more than a single analysis under these headings combining all products.

The chart will not actually pinpoint a particular fault – for example, giving a customer 15 per cent when he should really be in the 10 per cent bracket – nor would this fact necessarily be obvious from the invoices because a small dispatch normally qualifying for only 10 per cent discount might represent a part delivery of a larger order which had correctly qualified for 15 per cent discount. However, the chart will reveal any general trend towards larger discount. More usefully, it will also permit a cross-check of actual gross profit against forecast gross profit, which would not be possible without the information on discounts.

Sales made from stock

For wholesalers, retailers and stockholders generally, a record of sales orders received from customers should be identical with the invoices for goods dispatched. Although this would make a separation of the two sets of data superfluous, there remains the obstinate problem of orders which cannot be executed immediately because the goods required are not in stock.

Generally, a retailer would either ignore such orders, saying 'Sorry, sold out; try again next week', or would place specific orders on his suppliers to individual customers' requests.

With wholesalers and stockholders the position is different and calls for a close management grip on the action which falls into two sections:

1   Goods which it is not the firm's policy to hold in stock because demand is too small
2   Goods which were intended to be in stock but at present are sold out

Expenses of making sales

The expenses of making sales come in three main groups:

1   The basic fixed overhead expenses of the sales organisation
2   Variable costs of sales commissions
3   The costs of promoting sales by such means as advertising, direct mail, specials, bargain offers and other campaigns for attracting the attention of customers

The aim is not to keep these costs to the lowest possible absolute level but to keep them low relative to the volume of sales being made. Higher sales justify higher sales expenses. In some circumstances, they even justify expenses proportionately higher per unit sold.

Figure 6:4 shows the form recommended for calculating the effect of sales costs on net profit. This will indicate whether or not efforts at improving sales are successful. The combined effect of these changes may be forecast to ensure that they will lead to the desired extra net profit if the sales reach their target.

The variable selling costs listed would be those which depend mainly on the value of volume of sales for which in many firms the main item is the salesmen's commissions. The so-called fixed costs of the sales department are not really fixed but are liable to jump in large steps in the manner described under marginal costing in Chapter 8. These costs include:

1   Sales management salaries and related extras such as pension premiums and National Insurance contributions.
2   Sales clerical staff salaries and related extras
3   Basic fixed salaries of the sales staff
4   Sales office premises costs; rent, rates, heating, lighting, depreciation of fixtures and furniture
5   Sales records, equipment costs. Depreciation of mechanical aids to sales records
6   Stationery, postages and telephones for the sales department

7   Travelling and motor expenses for sales staff including depreciation of cars
8   Sales showroom costs

Detailed lists of these costs will be prepared each month as supporting data for the profit and loss account (Chapter 2). A useful accounting ratio is the proportion of fixed sales costs to the value of sales.

Credit Authorisation

Selling goods on credit creates two distinct problems of credit control for management:

1   Deciding in respect of each prospective customer whether to grant credit and if so to what limits; then, in due course, deciding whether to extend the limits when larger orders are received
2   Urging all customers to pay their accounts at the correct time, or at any rate as soon as possible after the due date

The decision to extend credit may call for a salesman's application for credit authorisation for a new customer. Many representatives prefer to have a 'hunch' that a customer will prove sound but management should require him to obtain some concrete facts and leave the decision to the credit controller or to the sales manager.

Figure 6:5 shows an example of a credit authorisation. Figure 6:6 shows an example of a form used for requesting an extension of agreed credit limit. In both cases the same form can be used as a request and for authorisation.

Accounts overdue

A summary total of current and overdue accounts serves little purpose, in spite of the popularity of the ratio of debtors to turnover. A careful study of a list of overdue accounts, shown in Figure 6:7, is a more practical approach to this problem.

This list can be prepared at the same time as the monthly statements, preferably within three working days of the end of the month. It will be used throughout the month to record the issue of reminder letters and the arrival of cheques in settlement of the accounts.

Number 1 reminder. This is in the form of a sticker or rubber stamp on the monthly statement.

Number 2 reminder. A standard polite reminder that the account is overdue and asking for early settlement.

These printed reminders carry little power so they should be followed up quickly by applications of a more personal nature. Telephone calls to customers' senior executives are usually more effective than letters.

Management should decide if they wish their representative to take any action to speed up the settlement of customers' accounts or whether they prefer to leave the matter in the hands of the credit controller. Generally, it is a good plan to involve the representatives, even though many of them dislike the duty. In any event, the representative must be kept informed about overdue accounts and the issue of reminders as it is pointless for salesmen to go coaxing for orders when the customer's account is giving cause for dissatisfaction. A copy of the overdue account list is satisfactory for this purpose, with the addition of a single letter code by each name to indicate the action. For example, *B* indicates that a number 2 routine reminder has been issued. *C* shows that the credit controller will telephone the customer to ask for settlement. *D* indicates that deliveries have been delayed until account is brought up to date.

A notice should be sent to the representative to keep him informed of activities.

> Please call on AB Limited of High Street, Newtown within the next week to press for payment of the overdue account. Alternatively, please confirm that you agree to the credit controller taking such action as may be necessary. Meanwhile, no further deliveries of goods are being made.

This notice is issued only when the delay has become serious. At earlier stages the code on the copy of the overdue account is adequate for keeping the representative informed. A copy is sent to the distribution warehouse to serve as the advice to them to discontinue deliveries.

A further notice must be sent to the representative and to the distribution warehouse when the customer's account has been brought up to date and he may again take deliveries.

> Your customer AB Limited has now paid its overdue account.

A copy of this is sent to the distribution warehouse to serve as advice to them to resume deliveries, but, if the past history of an account has been really bad or there is other cause to doubt that the customer is financially sound, the form will be clearly marked on both copies 'no more deliveries. Account closed.'

Notices issued to representatives are for confirmation and to avoid misunderstanding. They do not replace personal discussion.

A system may be introduced by which customers' orders are checked for credit control before being accepted into the manufacturing system or acknowledged to the customer. This involves keeping a record of orders already in hand as well as the balance on the ledger account.

Credit Controller's Action Programme

The credit controller should keep a diary similar to the one shown in Figure 6:8 with a different page for each day. Every day he should:

1   Mark off on the monthly list any cheques received in settlement of overdue accounts
2   Mark on the monthly list a record of telephone reminders and personalised letter reminders
3   Make an entry in the action programme against the appropriate day for further checking on the results from reminders. For example, if a customer says on 15 April 'I will pay within seven days,' this requires a check on 22 April whether his promise has been kept

Credit limits on ledger accounts

Each customer's ledger account will show the agreed credit limit on its heading. When the ledger clerk sees the balance has exceeded this limit, he will pass a written note to the credit controller.

```
                                            Date
            Advice from Ledger Office
                   to Credit Controller
            Customer's name _____
            Address _____
            This customer's account shows a balance of £
            compared with the credit limit of £
```

There may be valid reasons for the discrepancy, however. It could be, of course, that the account is not overdue but deliveries have been larger than usual. The credit controller has to decide on the action to be taken. This could be:

1   To restrict further deliveries until the balance has been reduced
2   To make inquiries with a view to raising the credit limit
3   To contact the customer and ask for a cheque

The main foundation for good credit control is to keep the sales ledger accounts right up to date.

Withdrawal of Credit Notice

Some firms use a standard form, as shown in Figure 6:9, for withdrawing credit. This form should be signed by the credit controller. The withdrawal of credit facilities is a drastic step likely to lead to permanent loss of a customer's business and should be issued only after careful assessment of the risk. However, when the facts justify this action, it should be taken firmly and credit should only be renewed after a careful review of the circumstances.

As a less drastic measure, dispatch of goods may be delayed when an account is overdue to bring pressure on the customer to settle his account and to avoid increasing the amount at risk.

With firms whose goods are custom-made to meet particular orders, it is important that the stopping of credit reflects right back to all orders in hand to avoid making goods only to find that they cannot be dispatched. This is particularly so with goods made to individual specifications which may be unsaleable if this one customer does not take them. In these circumstances, it might be pointless to withhold delivery of goods that have actually been made up. The need for extra care in accepting such orders is obvious and it makes the credit control more difficult. Close co-operation between credit controller and sales representatives is a great help and the credit controller is likely to get better results from a personal informal contact with the men than by issuing too many formal directives.

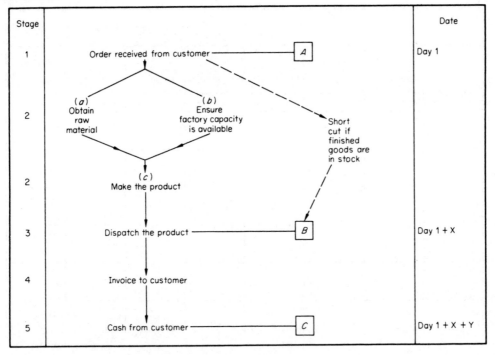

Figure 6:1   **Making and completing a sale**

UNITS					VALUE				
Forecast	50	30	40	20	140	£100	£90	£160	£80	£430
Product	*A*	*B*	*C*	*D*	Total	*A*	*B*	*C*	*D*	Total
Actual										
1 March	48	31	36	15	130					
2 March	56	35								
3 March	104	66								
4 March										
5 March										
(etc)										

Figure 6:2   **Record of goods invoiced to customers**

Date	Standard price per unit		Grade 2 customers 10% discount		Grade 3 customers 15% discount		Grade 4 customers 20% discount		Special with higher discounts		Total		Average per unit	
Period: month ending 31 March															
	Units	£	Units	£	Units	£	Units	£	Units	£	Units	£	Units	£
March 1	——	——	——	——	——	——	——	——	——	——	——	——	——	——
2														
3														

Figure 6:3   Analysis of discounts to customers

	Period 1 100 units	Period 2 150 units
Contribution (sales minus variable manufacturing costs) £x per unit		
—Fixed overhead costs of manufacturing and distribution		
—Fixed selling costs		
—Variable selling costs at £y per unit		
—Costs of promoting sales		
Net profit		

Figure 6:4   Analysis of effect of selling expenses

Customer's name

Address _____ Trade _____

Credit limit requested _____

Settlement terms _____

Details of premises _____

Details of trade _____

References

1 _____

2 _____

Representative _____

Trade credit report

Agency _____

Applied for _____
(date)

Credit authorisation _____

Maximum credit _____ Signature _____

Figure 6:5   Credit authorisation for new customer

GALVIN BROTHERS

Customer's name

II LONDON ROAD

Address

LONDON S W 13

Present credit limit £500

Revised limit requested £2000

History of account Trading since 1965. Average balance £450. Settlement always to correct time

Further references offered/requested None

Additional information Business appears to be thriving and is expanding to new branch premises

Revised credit limit £2000

Extension of credit authorised by B. Griffin

Figure 6:6   Request for extension of agreed credit limit

Accounts overdue at 31 March						
Customers	Total	March	Overdue			Comments
			One month	Two months	Three or more months	
AB Limited						Credit stopped action in hand
CD Limited						

Figure 6:7   Accounts overdue

Date		
Target	Actual	
3 April	5 April	Reference overdue account list and issue statements with number 1 reminders
10 April	11 April	Number 2 reminders
12 April	15 April	Start telephone reminders and personalised letter reminders

Figure 6:8   Credit controller's action programme

Customer_____

Address_____

No further goods are to be supplied to this customer until a fresh instruction is issued by the credit controller

Credit controller_____

Figure 6:9   Withdrawal of credit notice

7

Accounting for Labour

The urgency of daily supply of productive labour appears in the management accounting for the production departments. Equally important is the underlying structure by which employees are engaged, trained, brought into action and generally taken care of as valuable assets. Although the records in this connection will be for monthly rather than daily scrutiny, they deserve the same careful attention as is given to the statement of production and profit. The basic factors to be appreciated from the outset are:

1   The viewpoint of each individual employee is that the company exists to provide him with a job. He may be willing to forgo high earnings in favour of security or he may lack ambition to improve either himself or his usefulness, but still the dominant factor in his outlook is his own position as an employee. Here the motive of net profit, stressed as of prime importance in management accounting, must be overlaid by this personal attitude.

Management will see that the real interests of the company are so closely interwoven with those of the employees that the success or failure of each is dependent on the other. This is true for all grades and types of employees in factory, warehouse, office or sales department, including the managers themselves.

2   Even where automation has brought a very low ratio of staff to total factory production, the company is dependent on having the right people available at the right time. In fact, higher levels of skill and training needed for a relatively small staff, matched by high individual salaries, may make it doubly hard to correct the balance when the supply of employees goes out of line with the requirements.

3   Every department is affected by this topic.

Analysis of Skills

It is useful to have a fairly close definition of the kind of skill demanded for each position in the business and to attempt a similar definition of the skills possessed by each employee.

To illustrate this by an example familiar to most managers, it is convenient to look at typing. Duties may, for example, demand:

1   Copy typing, first quality
2   Copy typing, trainee quality
3   Audio typing, first quality
4   Audio typing, trainee quality
5   Shorthand typing, first quality
6   Shorthand typing, trainee quality
7   Shorthand typing, plus basic secretarial skills
8   Shorthand typing, plus senior secretarial skills
9   Typist/receptionist
10   Typist/telephonist
11   Typist with special accounting skills

In the very large companies, this division of typist into eleven categories is practical with corresponding salary structure. The smaller companies would be better suited with only two or three categories, having salaries fixed individually and a more rough and ready division of duties.

Yet even in the small firms the analysis is useful. It is wasteful financially to use a highly skilled senior shorthand typist for doing routine copy typing and boredom is likely to drive the girl to leave before long. On the other hand, for an executive to be asking for a junior trainee to turn out advanced work is frustrating to him and likely to be troublesome all round. One man in the company should be responsible for checking:

1   Which departments are creating essential work for typists
2   Which grades of typists are needed in each department and how many of them
3   That all needs are being met at optimum cost

This would be straightforward enough were it not for the fact that the situation is never static. Every week there are changes in both the staff available and the work required of them.

Typists are used here to illustrate the principles, but these comments would apply to every type of employee.

Manpower Planning Record

As with all management accounting, an eye to the future is of the utmost importance. The system should enable the various departmental managers and executives to co-operate with the personnel manager so that between them they can make sure that either:

1   Extra employees are on hand as required with suitable skill — or
2   Surplus employees are moved out into other departments

Figure 7:1 shows an example of a record used for comparing labour availability with future requirements. In a large company this statement may spread over several sheets. Abbreviation is scarcely possible, but a summary sheet, listing only the items showing a major surplus or deficit, should be useful.

The period covered by the forecast must depend on the nature of the business and of the work handled in the department. For unskilled work, in areas where labour is plentiful, a forecast one month ahead may be ideal. If the number of workers needed is going to increase, recruitment can begin and be completed at the right time, or, if the number needed is going down because the trade is seasonal or is at a low ebb for other reasons, redundancy procedures can be put in hand.

Disposing of surplus employees is no longer a matter of casually giving them notice. It calls for careful planning with 'natural wastage', transfers between departments and re-training for new skills all to be considered. This figure serves as an early warning of the need for putting these actions into effect.

Where labour is in short supply and/or training for particular duties is lengthy, the forecast may need to look further ahead, perhaps to three or six months; or two versions of the statement, one with a one-month and one with a six-month forecast may be needed.

The columns for surplus and shortage are the key ones for quick reference by senior management. In themselves, they say very little because they may hide a mass of detail, but they do pinpoint the trouble spots. They are set against the forecast rather than the current columns because the responsible manager will have taken a close look at his present position. He will have thought about how he can correct any existing difference between what is really needed and what is available and the forecast will show the revised position after making his planned adjustments.

This means that any surplus or shortage in the forecast is what still exists after making routine corrections. The present example illustrates this point. At present the department is four operatives below strength. Plans for recruitment or training are expected to bring the numbers up and the manager has taken the necessary action.

However, his needs are increasing to meet rising output and he has as yet no facilities for meeting this extra demand. His resources are stretched beyond their present limits.

Keeping the records up to date

Some employees may have several skills. Unfortunately, in practice, they are often prevented from using them because of the trade unions' 'demarcation of duties'. If the workers would realise that they, and not just the management and the country, lose by such foolish and shortsighted misuse of power, there would not be the frequent demands for legislation to bring the union trouble makers to heel.

Where flexibility is possible, an employee may have a preference to use skill A but is capable of exercising skill B when necessary to meet the company's temporary needs.

Such facts should be carefully shown in living records, not buried in long out-dated files. Manager X needs to know now, today, that this man is capable of filling his urgent need for a skill B operative. He cannot be expected to remember it in respect of the scores of staff involving dozens of skills. Even if he could remember, an assistant may be standing in while he is temporarily absent or his successor Y may have taken over as manager and easy reference is just as important as if X were on the spot.

Placing responsibility

In most companies, the departmental manager is the undoubted 'boss' of all the staff and operatives in his department. Where there is any danger of divided loyalties because a worker is in some way on loan from elsewhere — as, for example, a trainee student working through a succession of departments — any doubts about the allocation of his work should be carefully sorted out to forestall any difficulties.

Where the smaller firms rely on the departmental managers to take care of training, recruitment, wage negotiations and other details of employment, the preparation of this section of the management accounts will also be part of their duties. Such men are commonly under pressure of current work so that forward planning of personnel matters is starved of their attention.

By making up a statement once a month, even if only in shortened form, they will draw the attention of both themselves and the directors to any crisis that may be on the next horizon. This is ample reward for the small amount of time and trouble taken in preparing the statement.

For larger companies there is a division of responsibility between departmental manager and personnel manager. The personnel manager is the one most likely to be asked to prepare monthly statements and he will need information from the various managers when their needs are available.

Departmental Wage and Salary Summaries

For some departments the wages and salaries would remain constant in spite of variations in the company's sales or output. This would particularly be the case regarding employees whose earnings are classified in the accounts as part of the indirect overhead expenses; whereas wages for productive employees in the factory would be much more sensitive to changes in the volume of production.

One characteristic of these unchanging overheads is that beyond a certain point in the increase of business, they tend to move suddenly and violently upwards. They go up in large steps, becoming disproportionately costly at some stages. It is in their nature to show little inclination to reduce in response to a falling volume of business.

Figure 7:2 shows an example of a wages and salaries analysis by department, designed to draw management attention to the general level of this type of overhead expense. Such reports reinforce the presentation of the same facts in the manufacturing account (Chapter 1) and in the profit and loss account (Chapter 2) and indeed they are often the source of information for those accounts.

The report shown in Figure 7:2 is no more than a general warning. When it shows facts which are not satisfactory the management should look into the detail. Sweeping demands from the directors, such as 'Staff salaries in X department must be cut by 30 per cent. See to it!' are useless. It is more satisfactory to:

1 Ask for the reasons, assuming the departmental manager can find them.
2 Provide some skilled guidance for the departmental manager, such as bringing in the organisation and methods division to see where the system has gone wrong and where it should be put right

There is a wide range of ratios by which salaries and wages may be compared to output or sales. Some care is needed in choosing ones that are appropriate. Useful ratios could include:

1 Sales staff (representatives) as a percentage of sales
2 Sales staff (office personnel) as a percentage of sales
3 Factory staff as a percentage of the value of production which may be appreciably different from the value of sales if stocks are being built up or run down

Department—Production 3*SR* department						Date: 31 March			
Number of employees NOW		Classification	Forecast for 30 April				Wage rates (hourly/weekly)		
Needed	Available today		Needed	Available	Surplus	Deficit	Now £	At 30 April £	
30	26	Skill BS3MA BS3MT	35	30		5	0.80	0.85	

Figure 7:1   Analysis of labour comparing labour availability with requirements

						Period: month ending _____			
Budget		Department	Actual		Type	Ratios		Criticism	
Number of staff	£		Number of staff	£		Normal	Actual		
11	1000	*S*1 *S*2	9	895	1	7%	7.8%		

Figure 7:2   Wages and salaries analysed by departments

8

Standard Costing

A manufacturing company which is repeating similar activities regularly should prepare a list of standard costs for each stage. These standards will be founded on past experience and be modified according to changes such as the increase of wage rates or of other elements of cost. It is by no means essential for the products always to be identical. A variation of design or of ingredients from one product to another could fit very well into the system. For example, a standard rate of £1.80 per machine hour might be fixed and product A could have six machine hours costing £10.80 while product B had only five machine hours for £9.

Costs should be allocated to costs centres, a centre being an area under the control of one executive responsible for a department or activity. In this way the doctrine of personal responsibility is matched to the activity carried on within the department, to the spending in the same area and to the output achieved.

Programme for Standard Costing

There are several stages in setting up a standard costing system.

It is first necessary to decide the cost centres and list these each with its responsible executive and area of responsibility. Figure 8:1 shows an example of such a list.

In preparing the form it is necessary to decide on the items of expense relating to each centre and find the amount of each type of expense and the amount of production in the past year. Each executive should then be informed of his responsibilities. Figure 8:2 shows a typical memorandum from the managing director to a department head giving instructions on the records which must be produced and the intervals at which they are to be completed. A copy of this memo should be sent to any departmental manager who may be concerned with the costing programme.

It is feasible for the accounts department to prepare a schedule listing every action which must be taken each month, by whom and the date when the action must be taken. Figure 8:3 is an example of such a schedule. Forms must be designed to produce the data as required.

Actual results will then have to be compared with the standard for each period and an analysis be made of the standard and actual costs for each department to reveal any variances. Figure 8:4 shows an example of a form for doing this. Expenses from the separate records should then be summarised on one sheet to ensure that in total the separate records tally with the entire expenses of the whole business. Figure 8:5 shows a cross-check for the cost accountant to make. It only concerns the departmental managers where there are serious differences between the total of the separate records and the overall total. Sometimes this type of check reveals that some expenses have been overlooked from the costing system. Any variances should be shown as adverse or favourable.

Variances should be summarised and followed up with practical remedies. It is important, however, to allow for any known alterations which will make the coming year's expenses different. The standards to be applied to future production also need to be calculated. These will be used as guides (but not in themselves final decisions) to fixing selling prices and also as a basis for comparison of actual expenses.

Actual results should be compared with the standard each period. There are three approaches to adjust variances:

1   Amend the standards which have been proved wrong
2   Tighten up on the rate of spending which has been excessive
3   Speed up the rate of production which has been slack

These comments assume the actual results have been unfavourable but it is naturally possible that variances have proved to be to the company's advantage with production high and expenses low. In these circumstances credit for success is to be apportioned and again the standards may have to be changed for the future if the variances are likely to be permanent.

Budgetary control

It is in the area of costing, before all others, that principles of budgetary control have been most widely used. The existence of agreed standard costs and targets for output has been the ideal starting point for making a budget and a comparison of actual results forecast has belonged as much to budgetary control as to costing.

Budgetary control can exist without standard costing because it relates to other matters beside costing, but standard costing can scarcely exist without budgetary control, because a standard cost serves no purpose if the variances are not checked and explained and followed by suitable corrective action.

In the past a surprising number of firms have contented themselves with the preparation of standard costs, using them for fixing selling prices and overlooking the vital fact that if true costs are different from the standard, and no action is taken to put them right, the expected profit will not materialise.

Price Fixing

The price of each article being sold is fixed according to, or at least in the light of, the standard costs picked up from the cost centre lists. This ensures that no item of expense is overlooked or wrongly stated. A routine price fixing form should be devised with all cost centres listed in the left column. Figure 8:6 shows an example of price fixing analysis.

The details of the price per unit columns are then completed according to the facts discovered about the particular product. There is, for example, a standard charge per machine hour for work in production department 1, so it is only necessary to find the standard number of machine hours in order to complete the line for that department. Where the product misses a department completely there is a 'nil' entry which is safer than starting with a blank form and listing on it only those departments through which the particular product happens to pass. Elements of cost cannot be forgotten with this system.

The standard costs per machine hour for production department 1 might change at some time; this would be recorded and the facts be notified according to the time cycle shown in Figure 8:3. Alternatively, the amount of machine work might be found to be under or over-stated or the quantity or price of raw material might change. When there are more than two or three alternatives a fresh sheet would be drawn up and stapled to the front of the original which will be crossed through but not destroyed.

Selling prices are rarely fixed exactly in line with the standard costs plus agreed target profit margin. These costs merely serve as a close guide from which the sales director, with authorisation of the managing director, for a product selling in large quantities will decide on the actual selling price.

Decisions to accept selling prices below the level suggested by the costing system should be accepted only with reluctance and after the sacrifice has been carefully debated. Working with inadequate profit margins is an unsatisfactory way of doing business.

Fixing selling prices is a function of the directors, reflecting their skill and judgement. The standard costing system is a tool, providing them with useful help but it does not take away from the men the personal responsibility for the ultimate decision.

An article offered for sale is worth as much as it will fetch, taking into account the quantity it is desired to sell. If this price will not come up to the level demanded, if costs are to be covered and profit remain, the remedy is to make something different rather than to operate the business at a loss.

Marginal Costing

Where a company has several products, some selling more readily than others, and some more sensitive to a high selling price than others, it is useful to adopt marginal costing. It must be emphasised that this is not a substitute for standard costing but an additional exercise, serving a useful purpose.

For each product, a price-fixing sheet is prepared in the ordinary way, showing the standard costs and normal profit margin. A fresh set of figures for the marginal costs is then prepared for a group of products which match well together. The actual cost of production for one unit of any product will depend on:

1   The cost of raw material and the wages directly used making it up, with any other costs relating directly to the single unit – plus
2   A share of the overhead expenses. Above the cost the company will wish to earn some profit in arriving at the selling price

In the standard costing system each type of cost was calculated from an agreed scale and a regulation percentage was added for the profit. However, this was modified in arriving at the actual selling prices with the effect that a different profit from the standard level was made and this could be either above or below the standard.

Alternatively, a selling price might be cut with the object of selling more units, obtaining a smaller margin of profit from each unit and arriving at a larger final profit. In marginal costing:

1   Any costs which are fixed and cannot be attributed precisely to any specific product are listed as fixed costs
2   For each different product the costs *directly* attributable to the product are listed as variable costs. These include in particular the raw materials and direct wages
3   The selling price is settled according to market conditions with only a passing reference to the facts shown by the normal standard costing system
4   The product makes a 'contribution' towards the fixed costs and towards the profit. This contribution is simply the difference between the selling price and the variable costs. For example, product *AB* has variable costs for material £2.50 plus direct wages £1 equals total variable cost £3.50; the selling price of £6 leaves a contribution towards fixed costs and profit of £2.50

There is no serious attempt to make the contribution from this product bear the same relationship to variable costs or to selling price as is made by other products. The theory is that provided the total contribution from all products is large enough, the final outcome will be satisfactory in having covered all costs and left an adequate net profit.

Formula.   The theory of contribution may be extended by using a simple formula:

$$S - V = F + P$$

S is sales (number of units *x* selling price per unit)
V is variable costs (number of units *x* variable costs per unit)
F is fixed costs (total figure)
P is profit (net before tax)

When any three of the factors are known, it is possible to calculate the fourth.

The most obvious problem is to find the profit when the other three factors have been worked out, but there are variations. The selling price is fixed by external market conditions. Company investment policy demands a minimum profit of £*x*. Fixed costs are already established. One must then establish the quality that the company can afford to build into the product, according to the amount which can be spent on variable costs if the equation is to balance. The number of units could possibly be changed. This would lead to different figures for *S* and *V* but keeping the same variable cost and selling price per unit.

The establishment which makes the fixed costs inevitable could conceivably be diversified and part of it put to other uses, so that fixed costs chargeable against this activity could be reduced. In this case it would be necessary to prepare a graph using the marginal costing approach. An example of such a graph is shown in Figure 8:7.

Marginal costing as a guide to safety

With a normally full level of production the standard costing system sets an agreed proportion of profit to the value of sales. When the volume of output varies either above or below the normal level, the profit does not change by straight multiplication of the standard profit per unit by the number of units over or under produced.

The change in profit is, in fact, considerably more violent than this because it depends on the change in contribution, as shown by the marginal costing system. A selling price may be cut with the object of selling more units; obtaining a smaller margin of contribution from each unit and arriving at a larger final profit. Figure 8:8 shows the different alternatives compared and the results.

Figure 8:9 shows a similar form for analysing three products, using standard costing and marginal costing. The principle here is to see that each product makes a contribution towards the fixed costs and profit, without being emphatic that contributions must always be proportionate to costs. The size of the contribution will depend on three factors:

1   The difference between variable costs and selling price per unit – and

2   The volume of sales of each different kind of product — and
3   Possibly, the total volume of production

Where there is a choice between arranging costs, so that they are variable rather than fixed, the result will be to make the company less vulnerable to a drop in output but able to benefit less when output is above target. Security is bought in exchange for a chance to show exceptionally good (or bad) results.

It is in the nature of some industries to be obliged to have a high proportion of fixed to variable costs whereas other industries have a lower proportion. Within the range which is natural to a particular kind of industry, management may choose variable in place of fixed by obtaining as many services as possible from outside companies, paying for them on a basis for £x per unit or £y per job. Examples are packaging, delivery (haulage contractors rather than own fleet of vehicles), specialist services (such as accounting, technical advice and work study), put out work (instead of own employees) and buying components ready made, etc.

Alternatively, a company which has deliberately aimed for a high proportion of fixed costs or is stuck with a situation in which a high proportion is almost inevitable, will need to buy security by making as sure as possible that sales and output always equal or exceed the standard target. This assumes that security is desirable for itself and not all directors agree that this is the case. In this way, they stand to reach the benefits of an increase without often being hit by the consequences of a fall in output or sales. This objective is achieved by either or both:

1   Deliberately basing the standard well within the firm's capacity for making and selling. The snag is that prices will not be competitive
2   Having a sales force stronger than is really needed for the available factory capacity, so that in a period when selling is difficult there will still be sufficient orders to keep the factory busy. Snags are, first, when selling is easy the orders will exceed available productive capacity (in some firms this may be made good by asking other companies to manufacture the goods to meet the extra demand) and, second, the cost of the over large selling force will be high

The preparation of a simple statement each accounting period, comparing actual results, as in Figure 8:9, with standard target results, draws attention to the benefits of having exceeded the target or to the loss of profit because of having failed to reach the target.

Detailed inspection of the underlying facts is necessary to find out whether the difference between target and actual was caused by the failure of the factory to produce or of the sales force to secure orders.

Break-even Charts

The opening sections of this chapter have supposed that a clear-cut line could be drawn between costs which were variable in direct proportion to quantity of production, or of sales, and those which were fixed regardless of sales. If this were the case it would be a fairly simple matter to construct a break-even chart to discover the anticipated profit with various levels of sales. Figure 8:10 is an example of such a chart.

In this example the variable costs are superimposed above the fixed costs. Where they meet the line showing value of sales is the break-even point at which there is no profit or loss.

It might be decided to increase the quantity of sales by reducing all selling prices. This would call for a new sales line to be drawn at a less steep angle. However, if sales up to X units were at normal selling prices and only additional sales were made at cut prices, the original line would be correct up to the point at which price per unit was reduced.

In practice, none of the costs are perfectly variable and none are absolutely fixed. The movement of the costs is erratic.

If progressive reductions in selling prices were offered to selected customers, the result would be a curving line for the sales. Beyond a certain point, it is found that additional sales make no further addition to the profit because they are not greater than their own variable costs. This becomes obvious from Figure 8:11 where the line for sales is drawing gradually closer to the line for variable costs as it proceeds across the right side of the graph.

At a still lower selling price per unit, when selling price has dropped below the variable costs of those extra sales, each additional sale makes an outright reduction in profit and a sales effort has been a positive disservice to the company.

A graph such as this should be prepared each month or each time there is discussion on changing selling prices and/or quantities sold, in order to project the effect if actual sales prove to be greater or less than the budgeted level.

Overheads analysis

Each different kind of overhead expense is subject to the same difficulty of reaching saturation point and needs to be supplemented by additional facilities which come fairly expensive.

The stages at which a sharp rise in overheads is unavoidable do not all come at the same point for different kinds of expense. For example, one typist might be needed to issue 1000 units per period, but a second typist would have to be engaged if output went above 1100 units. This would mean the cost per unit for typing invoices would rise steeply at this point. It would be a comparatively simple matter to engage a part-time employee or someone handling invoices plus other duties, of course. The problem is to assess the point at which the steps will occur and their height, neither of which is easy.

Plotting overhead costs

Assuming the additions to 'fixed' overheads may be made with reasonable accuracy, it is possible to plot their effect and produce a graph showing two or more optimum levels of output to yield maximum profit, as is shown in Figure 8:12. The advantage of this type of graph is to help to decide when it is better to let sales demand outstrip production, leaving potential customers unsatisfied, rather than add a large indivisible chunk of extra overheads to meet a small extra demand for present capacity.

There are many management factors to watch when deciding on changes in output capacity. These include:

1   The existing factory/warehouse/sales unit may appear to be a physical one to which a simple addition of space, buildings and machinery will create an extension. In reality, the unit is a group of people working harmoniously together; the fact of 'harmonious' being proved by the success which has pushed output up to meet capacity and has suggested the further increase in facilities.

The extension may include engaging new staff and changing various people's working routines and their daily environment. At the same time the management will become a stage more remote from the production workers and office staff because they will have a larger area of duties and a wider physical area to control. This introduces personal problems and it will become necessary to establish a new unit of people not merely an extra one or two people in the existing unit. This is a matter which cannot be measured primarily in financial terms nor can it be ignored because it is fundamental to the success of the whole business.

2   A decision to delay increasing production capacity and turn away potential customers may be sound from an immediate profit point of view but those frustrated customers will turn their demand to other companies which may respond only too strongly by stepping ahead of this company and starting to encroach on its existing sales area as well as meeting the demand from those whose orders it has neglected.

This again is not easily reduced to straight financial terms. It is pointless to expand slightly on to unprofitable levels of output if the sales would remain at that rate indefinitely. On the other hand, it may be sound long-term planning to take a temporary cut in profit for a few months as a consequence of extending production facilities if sales would then later build up to an even higher level at which those new items could be fully employed and so show an even larger profit than ever before.

3   A decision to expand would involve a fresh review of whether adequate funds are available (Chapter 4) and whether enough employees can be engaged and trained (Chapter 5). The senior management must examine these points with the optimum output chart and they may decide that an output level other than optimum may be necessary because of the restraints due to funds and staff.

Centre number	Department	Responsible executive	Area of responsibility
1	Purchasing	Smith	Buying raw materials Stock control in the raw materials warehouse
2	Production *A*	Jones	
3	Production *B*	Robinson	
4	Production *C*	Brown	
5	Distribution	Johnson	
6	Accounting	Thomas	
7	Administration	Jackson	
8	Personnel	Kent	
9	Sales	Speight	
(etc)			

Figure 8:1   Example of a list of cost centres

M E M O R A N D U M

From Managing Director   Date 10 April 1981

To   Mr. A J Smith Chief Purchasing Officer

COSTING PROGRAMME

Two main areas of cost are within your responsibility. These are:

1 The buying prices for all raw materials, components and other purchases, including basic prices,

   trade discounts and bulk buying terms.

2 The expenses of running the purchase activity, including the ordering and acceptance of goods and

   the raw materials warehouse; wages for warehouse employees and salaries for office staff; costs

   of the premises and mechanical handling plant and warehouse equipment.

The actual costs for the month ending 31 March 1981 are listed on form 123. The revised figures

forecast for the month to 31 May 1981 are on form 456 and they will serve as the standard costs

for that period. In due course the actual costs for May will be produced by the cost accounting

staff, together with a note of any variance.

You are requested to help with the regular control of costs by:

1 Notifying the cost accounting department each time you know of any alteration in any of the

   items in either 1 or 2 above. These changes will affect the standard costs and on some

   occasions they may result in changing selling prices or sales promotion plans. The earlier

   the costing staff learn of any such changes, the sooner the appropriate adjustments can be made.

   Please do not wait until the month is complete before dealing with these.

2 By preparing a memo each month, when variances from standard costs are listed for you by the cost

   accounting staff, in order to show the causes of variance and the action you propose taking.

Figure 8:2   Example of a costing programme

Day of month	Action	Action by	Example of dates
6th	Summary of actual costs and variances for previous month	Cost accounting staff	6 April for March actual costs
9th	Memo on the causes of variance and consequential proposals for remedies or changes	Executive responsible for cost centre	9 April for March results leading to future changes
12th	Discuss the memo and authorise the executive to go ahead with the remedies he suggests or with suitable adjustments	Managing Director	12 April for earliest possible action
15th	Draft list of standard costs for the coming month	Cost accounting staff on basis of discussions with executive responsible for cost centre	15 April for the May programme
20th	Agreed final list of standard costs for the coming month	Cost accounting staff	20 April for May programme
Every day	A note of any known changes in costs or in other factors affecting standards	Executive responsible for cost centre notifies cost accounting staff	Any day
Any day	A memo commenting when major cost changes mean a significant alteration in profit margins or call for review of selling prices	Chief cost accountant	Any day
Any day	A review of selling prices or other production levels in consequence of the memo notified as above	Meeting of directors and departmental managers who may be affected by the topic	
25th	Notify managing director that plans agreed on 12th day have been put in hand	Executive responsible for cost centre	

Figure 8:3   Cost centre schedule

Department : Purchasing and Raw Materials Warehouse		Date : 20 April for May 1981	
Executive responsible : A J Smith, Chief Purchasing Officer		Budget : _____	
Standard costs	First section—Raw materials and components	Actual costs	Variances
£2.35 per unit 10% discount for bulk of 1000 units or 12½% for 8000 units	Raw Material PQ Grade 2/S		
	All the important materials will be listed		
£ £	Second section—Departmental costs	£ £	
	Management salaries 3 men Standard 20% addition for extras separately detailed Warehouse wages 6 men 2 juniors Standard 20% addition for extras Clerical staff salaries Office accommodation – rent rates insurance heating and lighting Raw materials Warehouse accommodation (etc)		

Figure 8:4   Standard costs and variances form

Department	Type of expense			Month ending: _____
From separate records				
	Insurance	Rates	Etc	
1	200	260		
2	340	190		
3	270	310		
4	430	350		
(etc)				
Total	1240	1110		
Actual overall	1290	1100		
Difference	50	10		
Action required	Detailed checking	none		

Figure 8:5   Cross-check on total of separate records against whole of business expenses

Product _2B4_		Date _1 March_

Cost centres	Detail	per unit
Purchasing—raw material	£ 1% addition for departmental costs £	
Components—1	£ 1% addition for departmental costs £	
	£ 1% addition for departmental costs £	
Production department 1	6 machine hours at £ per hour	
Production department 2	2 machine hours at £ per hour	
Production department 3	Nil	
Distribution	Export sale, actual cost addition for departmental costs	_____
Selling	20%	_____
Administration and accounting	Addition for general overheads	
	plus 20%	_____
	Profit 10%	_____
	Guide to selling price	_____

Actual selling price fixed in light of all known circumstances of the market £_____

Document prepared by	Selling price authorised by
J. White	_B Speight_
Cost accountant	Sales manager

Figure 8:6   Price-fixing analysis

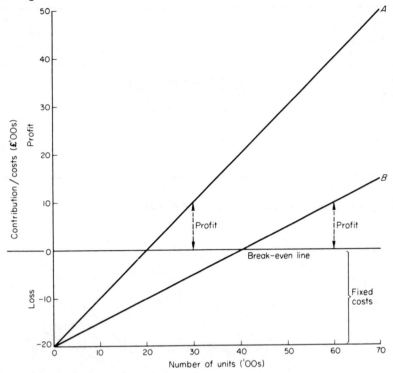

Figure 8:7   Graph using the marginal costing approach

	A	B	C	D
Units sold	100	120	200	140
Selling price £	10	8	5	8
Variable costs at £3 per unit £	300	360	600	420
Sales value £	1000	960	1000	1120
Contribution £	700	600	400	700
Fixed costs £	500	500	500	500
Profit £	200	100	—	200
Loss £	—	—	100	—

Figure 8:8   Comparison of sales and profit

Product	Budget			Actual			Totals	
	A	B	C	A	B	C	Budget	Actual
Units sold	250.00	70.00	40.00	200.00	50.00	20.00	360.00	270.00
Variable costs per unit £	30.00	30.00	30.00	30.00	30.00	30.00		
Selling price £	75.00	100.00	120.00	75.00	100.00	120.00		
Sales value £'000	18.75	7.00	4.80	15.00	5.00	2.40	30.55	22.40
Variable costs £'000	7.50	2.10	1.20	6.00	1.50	0.60	10.80	8.10
Contribution £'000	11.25	4.90	3.60	9.00	3.50	1.80	19.75	14.30
Fixed expenses £'000							14.40	14.40
Profit £							5.35	—
Loss £							—	0.10

Figure 8:9   Comparing sales of three products and effect on profit

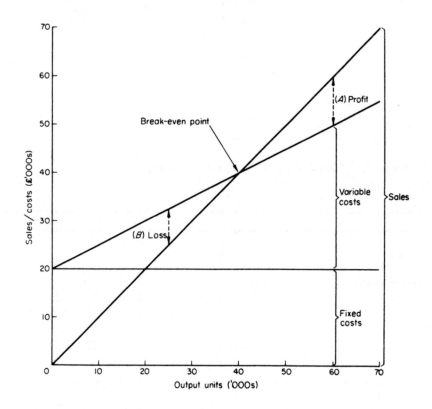

Figure 8:10   Simple break-even chart

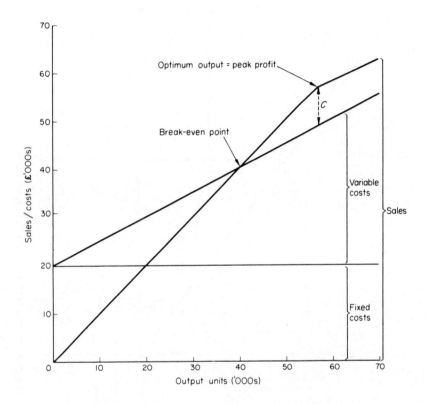

Figure 8:11   Break-even chart with different selling prices

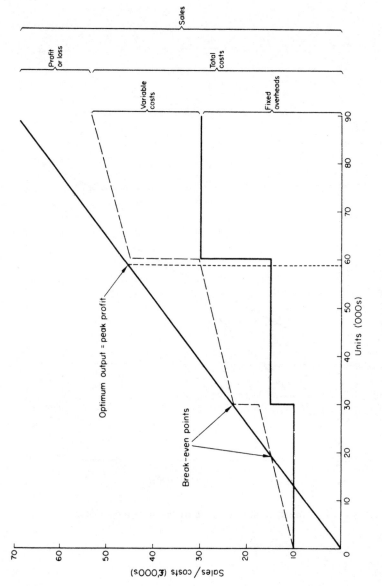

Figure 8:12 Stepped overheads and optimum output chart

9

Investment Appraisal

To acquire 'correct' fixed assets as original equipment or replacements is an important part of the management control of most industrial companies. Correct decisions lead to:

1   The ability to make the product at the speed required, to the quality required
2   The chance to compete on favourable terms with other companies
3   Optimum operating and maintenance costs

— and so to high net profit. Wrong decisions lead to:

1   Surplus assets standing idle or inadequate assets overworked and not meeting the demand for products
2   Heavy operating and maintenance costs
3   The choice between sacrificing the unsuitable assets in favour of better replacements or keeping them and continuing to operate in unsatisfactory conditions

— and so to net loss (or unnecessarily low net profit). The plan recommended is to set up a system of making forecasts of future needs, assessments of the correct assets to meet those needs, and an appraisal of the standard assets to judge whether they will continue to serve.

These are essentially technical matters to be dealt with by the skilled managers of departments and the senior executives with suitable practical knowledge. Only such men, as distinct from accountants, can take the mixture of known facts about the assets and forecasts of the future to give a correct solution.

Investment appraisal and capital expenditure budgeting bring together the facts and informed opinions of the technical experts in ways that will help the directors to make correct decisions about the company's fixed assets. They will know when to make additions or replacements, how much to spend, how to balance the plant and buildings to the available raw material/labour/funds/outlets for products and other factors.

The point being stressed is that correct technical judgement is nine-tenths of the work of investment appraisal and budgeting. The DCF calculation, or other appropriate management accounting technique, is merely the final one-tenth of the process. If faulty or careless judgement is used in the first nine-tenths, the end result must be wrong. When non-accountant executives understand this, and especially if they are willing to learn the theory behind the final one-tenth, they can see the real importance of their own contribution to the forecasts. Questions commonly to be answered include:

1   Will additional plant, machinery and buildings be needed in the coming period to meet the rising demand for the company's products?
2   Are additional products under consideration? These would each have to be assessed as a whole with their demand for new plant/buildings/employees/sources of material/markets for disposal of the product leading to their contribution to net profit
3   Are existing machines in need of replacement or would extensive repairs to the old ones be more satisfactory?
4   When a decision has been reached that new machines are needed, should they be acquired by purchase, hire purchase or lease?

Forecast of Fixed Assets

It is useful to prepare a simple list of those assets which have been through the process of appraisal and have received management approval in principle. Final authorisation may not have been given, because only when the entire needs have been assembled can the management judge whether the firm's resources can meet the demand. For example, funds may be in short supply or if a big new venture is planned, its start might depend, until the very last possible moment, on assessment of national (or international) market conditions.

Figure 9:1 is an example of a simple list giving a forecast of fixed assets. The list has two parts: part 1 lists fresh items added since the previous list was prepared and part 2 those items already reviewed and authorised in the previous list. The items in part 2 will have been ordered and so are already a positive commitment which cannot be cancelled without difficulty, but it remains part of the forecast and is needed to help show the total position. .

Items could be entered according to departments so that deliveries due in a department in October, say, will appear before those due next August in another department. Alternatively, all items for one month for all departments could appear before any of those for the following month. However, to keep everything for one department together, regardless of dates, is generally more convenient.

Where a major new project is to start, which could involve every department in adding to its existing assets, it may be better to keep this project separate in a block by itself rather than mix it with other more routine matters.

Future commitments mean additional regular expenses because of acquiring this asset. It would not apply to mere replacements of existing assets, as the cost of running the whole would already be a part of the monthly revenue expenses. Details of the future commitments would be given in supplementary notes as there is not space to list them on this sheet.

Every department should submit a set of figures for entry on this simple list every month. Nil returns should be made where there are no fresh entries, to make certain that the preparation of a forecast has not merely been overlooked.

Forecast of Contribution to Income and Expenditure

The steps leading up to a decision on whether to acquire an additional asset begin with a list of the main facts, some being positive and others to be estimated by the departmental manager. A suitable questionnaire such as the one shown in Figure 9:2, should be drawn up to make sure all matters are remembered and taken into consideration.

When a machine is to replace money or labour, the cut in wages will be entered as equivalent to income, but under a separate heading to distinguish it from true income. If there will be redundancy problems, these should be mentioned as they involve both exceptional expense and personnel problems. It is not necessary to do a separate list for each individual asset. Where a whole group of assets are needed for a new project, a single list combining them all will be suitable.

Cash Flow Statements

The next step is to produce cash flow statements, setting out the income and expenditure in chronological order. After the initial heavy expense, if the income is running monthly at about the same pace as the expenditure, it is fairly satisfactory to do the list on a once-a-year basis, making the entries as if all the income and all the spending took place at the end of each year. However, if there are quite wide seasonal variations, so that the flow of either income or expenditure is very uneven, it is necessary to make four quarterly entries for each year and to use discounting with quarterly instead of annual tables. The difference between this and annual entries will be found to be quite large, in some cases large enough to affect a decision on whether or not to go ahead and buy the asset.

Statement of expenditures

Figure 9:3 shows an example of a cash flow statement of expenditures. Details of the routine costs would appear in the sheet shown in Figure 9:2.

The tax included on this form would be the corporation tax on the profit expected to be created by the project, ignoring capital allowances which are better treated as a separate item. The company has a standard delay of between nine and twenty-one months from the completion of each year's profit and the due date of payment of the tax. For example, tax on profit for the year ending 31 December 1980 might be due for payment on 31 December 1981. So tax on the 1980 profit will appear as outgoing cash against the year of the project nearest to 31 December 1980.

Statement of income

A separate cash flow statement for income also has to be completed. The form shown in Figure 9:4 is typical of a cash flow statement of income. The executive responsible for this forecast may need to refer to the accountant for details of capital allowances for which there are several different scales. The three scales of most common interest to industrial companies are:

1   *Industrial buildings; new buildings.* The 1975 Finance Act increased the initial allowance to 50 per cent. Writing down allowance, 4 per cent of the original cost each year, including the first year. Balancing allowance or balancing charge if the building is sold before being completely written off. This balancing figure brings the total allowances equal to net cost (purchase price minus grant minus resale price). The balancing charge will not be greater than would cancel the allowance already received.

Used buildings. 'Residue of original expenditure' is spread over the remainder of twenty-five years or of fifty years for buildings which were new before November 1962.

2   *Scientific expenditure on research and development.* The whole cost qualifies for capital allowances in the year of purchase.

3   *Plant and machinery.* The first year allowance is 100 per cent of the cost price of the asset. A smaller first year allowance may be claimed if preferred, followed by a writing down allowance in subsequent years equal to 25 per cent of the written down value.

Discounted cash flow statement

The next step is to discount the cash flow at the company's target rate. This is done by preparing a summary of the income and expenditure taken from Figure 9:3 and 9:4 to calculate the net present value after taking into account the discount factor, as is shown in Figure 9:5. The object of this move is to discover whether the project will meet the minimum level of return which the management have decided in order to regard any activity as worth undertaking.

Where the total of the net present value is positive, the target has been exceeded and the project is satisfactory. If the total had been negative, the asset would not be worth buying because it would not make an adequate return on the investment.

A decision on the correct percentage to use for the discount factor is a responsibility for the directors. The choice is a matter of alternatives which are:

1   The rate should not be so high that no projects can ever reach it
2   It should not be so low that it leaves no greater profit than could be obtained from a risk free investment in government securities. Most firms would regard 10 per cent as a compromise, noting that this is after corporation tax

There are many other theories of investment appraisal but there seems to be little point in using more than one. Net present value is suitable as it leads to the required information.

Capital Gains Tax Roll Over Deferment Record

One further refinement is needed where the problem is to select between two or more different projects which would have different lengths of life. For this the annual value must be calculated as in Figure 9:6.

This is a continuing record of capital gains tax roll over deferment which should be retained permanently and scrutinised at least once in every six months. Where the relationship between a sale and a purchase is in danger of exceeding the twelve month time limit, a monthly review is needed.

Capital Gains Tax

When the company sells a fixed asset for more than its original cost, there may be a liability to capital gains tax which is payable at the same rate as corporation tax and becomes an inclusive part of the corporation tax demand.

Apart from the effect of this tax on the profit and cash flow calculations, where they will not be separated from the main corporation tax, they may also be relevant to management accounting with their scope for roll over deferment. This deferment may result in the tax being postponed indefinitely, so long as the replacement asset is retained. Alternatively, if the replacement is a wasting asset the deferment will terminate after a maximum of ten years, or sooner if the replacement asset is sold in less than ten years. There is an exception to this if the replacement asset is itself in its turn replaced by a fresh permanent asset, in which case the deferment may be renewed and may continue indefinitely. For deferment to apply the replacement must be bought not more than twelve months before the original asset is sold nor more than twelve months after it has been sold. This gives a two-year spread and creates a need for careful comparison of the list of purchase and sales of fixed assets. The time limit may be extended at the discretion of the Inspector of Taxes and the management should ensure that suitable requests for extension of time limit should be submitted before the time limit itself has run out. The request should be accompanied by an explanation of the reason for the delay in completing the matching transaction.

Cash Value

Cash value of the capital allowance is equal to their amount multiplied by the percentage at which tax is payable. For example, if a first year allowance of 100 per cent on an asset costing £1000 is claimed and if corporation tax is 52 per cent, this has a cash value of £1000 x 52 per cent which equals £520.

Delay

The cash value of the first capital allowances appears in the cash flow statement against the year in which tax is payable on profit created during the year in which the asset was bought.

For example, if the accounts are made up annually to 31 December with tax payable one year later, a machine bought at any time during 1980 would effectively take capital allowances to be entered in the cash flow against 31 December 1981.

Example.   A machine bought between 1 January 1980 and 31 December 1980 in a company making up its accounts to 31 December. First year allowance 100 per cent of £1000. Profit from other projects for 1979 is £10 000 on which tax at 52 per cent is £5200 but these capital allowances may be deducted, £1000, leaving taxable profit at only £9000 on which tax at 52 per cent is £4680. So the capital allowances have been equivalent to extra income of £520, which is the amount by which they have cut the demand for tax payable on 1 January 1982, equals 31 December 1981.

If costs at first are greater than income the capital allowances can be used against profit created on the company's other existing projects so that they can become effective before the new project is profitable. Where there are no profits from other sources, the capital allowances are deferred and become effective when taxable profits are available.

Insurance Records

The business must have insurance and the directors should regard it as a management problem to be settled under the following headings:

1   Cover is to be arranged for each different kind of risk or a conscious decision taken to leave some kinds of risk without cover
2   Renewal cover with revision of insured values is to be arranged at regular intervals or when the occasion arises
3   Claims are to be made

One executive should be made clearly responsible for looking after all insurance matters. In smaller firms it will probably be the owner or managing director but in larger companies the duty may be passed to the company secretary, or some other executive. The great thing is that everyone, including the man himself, should know exactly who is looking after insurance, then, when there is any incident calling for insurance action, they can make sure that the right man is aware of it.

Only rarely will this individual have any technical knowledge of insurance but this is not of serious consequence. If he does have knowledge so much the better, but otherwise he has plenty of opportunities to ask for expert advice at the right times. This expert advice is always freely available:

1   Business may be placed direct with one of the insurance companies
2   The company may use a firm of insurance brokers

There are two advantages in going direct to an insurance company. First, the insurance company has its own qualified specialists who will give really sound, professional advice when cover is being arranged. Second, they may be prepared to offer some discount on premiums if all types of insurance are being placed with them. Against this, there tends to be a slight feeling that no one is taking our side when claims arise.

The benefits claimed for going to a broker are that he will shop around for the best terms for each kind of policy and he will give professional advice. With the better firms of brokers, these points are perfectly true and they will also lean very strongly in the client's favour in helping to get fair settlement of difficult claims. However, it is not practical to push the whole matter of insurance on to the brokers. The firm's own executive must still keep the brokers informed about changes in the risks and follow up claims as they arise.

The management accounts will include insurance under the headings of premiums paid and claims.

Insurance record – premiums

Figure 9:7 shows an example of a record of insurance premiums. This summary should be well supported by supplementary sheets giving full details of the policies. For example, the directors will need to know that consideration has been given to up-dating the amount of cover on each different kind of risk. They will need to see the amount insured last year and the change that has taken place during the last twelve months.

In the smaller companies there is much to be said for having all insurance premiums renewable on the same date and preferably with the same insurance company. Thus it is one single task to examine the whole of the insurance risk and bring the whole thing up to date. In the larger companies it may be more practical to have the renewals spread through the year as there will be sufficient work to keep one man regularly busy looking after the insurance matters throughout the year and it is better for his work to be spread than to be bunched up all together.

Insurance record – claims

It is a surprisingly easy matter for claims to be left outstanding for so long by the insurance companies that they are eventually completely forgotten. By keeping one detailed page in hand in respect of each claim and not removing it from the files until the claim has been settled this risk of the claim being forgotten is eliminated. Figure 9:8 is an example of a claims record.

The insurance executive may also contact the directors regarding the disposal of assets which have been damaged and have been the subject of an insurance claim but remain available for disposal for whatever price they will fetch.

Uninsured losses may, on some occasions, be recoverable from third parties. This is particularly the case with motor claims; the company's insurance executive may enlist the support of a solicitor or of the insurance company in pursuing claims of this nature against the third parties.

		List as at _31 March_				
Part 1: Additions to list since _28 February_						
Department	Description of fixed asset	Date due for delivery	Date due for payment	Cost price	Future routine commitments	Addition or replacement
A	4C cutting machine	June 1981	July 1981	£6000	see note 3	A
B	T5B truck	Aug 1981	Sept 1981	£1500	–	R
Part 2: Items already reviewed and authorised in earlier lists						

Figure 9:1   Forecast of fixed assets

Department A ASSET: 4C cutting Machine

              Description: Mills-Stewart large size

How much will it cost: | £ | £ |
                                                                |---|---|

      to buy

      to operate—running costs—wages
                            fuel
                            etc

                  maintenance—approximate average for 1st year
                                                    2nd year
                                                    3rd year
                                                     (etc)

            any other outgoings

                                                    Total

How long will it last? _____

Will it have any re-sale value at the end of its economic working life? Estimate £_____

Will it qualify for capital allowances? _____

Will it qualify for any investment or other kind of grant?_____

INCOME: How much will it bring into the firm: _____

1 by way of direct income _____

2 by reducing existing costs _____

Figure 9:2   Forecast of contribution to income and expenditure

Year	Cost of asset	Other routine costs	Tax	Total
0				
1				
2				
3				
4				
5				
Total				

Figure 9:3 Cash flow statement — expenditure

Year	Sales income	Capital allowances	Incidental income	Total income
0				
1				
2				
3				
4				
5				
Total				

Figure 9:4 Cash flow statement — income

Year	Income	Expenditure	Cash flow	Discount factor 10%	Net present value
0		6000	−6000	1.000	−6000
1	5400	1500	+3900	0.909	+3545
2	5240	3200	+2040	0.826	+1685
3	5140	3200	+1940	0.751	+1456
4	5100	3200	+1900	0.683	+1297
5	1000	1200	− 200	0.621	− 124
	£21 880	£18 300	+£3580		+£1859

Figure 9:5 Discounted cash flow statement

SALES					PURCHASES				Deferment check	
Sale number	Date	Details	Sale price	Capital gain	Purchase number	Date	Details	Cost price	Sale number	Purchase number
1	3.8.81	Warehouse in K Street	£12 000	£3000	1	3.4.82	Land in T Road	£4000	1	1
					2	12.6.82	Building on T Road land	£3000	1	2

Figure 9:6   Record of capital gains tax roll over deferment

Date due	Policy number	Type of policy	Risk covered	Department chargeable	Net amount of premium	Notes (e.g. no-claim discounts)
		Fire Theft Motor Employer's liability Public liability Consequential loss				

Figure 9:7   Insurance record — premiums

Date of loss or accident	Policy Number	Type	Brief detail of claim	Amount	Notes (e.g. uninsured losses through under-insurance
6.5.81	2489	Fire	Fire damage at K street warehouse	£2800	Settlement promised for 30 June will leave £500 not recoverable

Figure 9:8   Insurance record — claims

10

Stock Holding and Purchasing

Recording the quantities and values of stock may be regarded as an exercise in its own right but making use of the figures crosses over into the area of management accounting.

To produce the monthly statement of profit, which is a central feature of the management accounting, it is essential to have certain facts about the stock:

1   The value of closing stock at either cost price or the price used in the valuation as at the start of this period
2   How much must be written off the value in 1 to arrive at the present market value of the stock
3   The final value after deducting 2 from 1

The figure in 1 refers to raw material and will be used in the manufacturing account to arrive at the cost of raw material used in manufacture during the period. A separate deduction will then be made from the raw material figure equal to item 2.

The same approach should be used for the value of the work in progress. In the trading account the amount shown in 1 relating to the stock of finished goods should be used with a separate deduction for 2.

The purpose of this distinction of the figures is to enable the management to judge the effectiveness of manufacture and of trading separately from the losses due to the falling value of the stock. Sometimes the stock losses are outside the company's control and at other times they are caused by the errors of judgement, or inefficiency, of executives other than the men directly responsible for the factory or the trading policy.

The stock figure as in 3 after deducting reductions in value, would be used as the opening figure for the next period in both the forecast and the actual so that last month's troubles would not be the cause of a repeat of the same investigation next month. For each period it is only the stock troubles of that one period which are under scrutiny.

In some trades a reduction in stock value is accepted as inevitable. It will be taken into the forecast so that only a variation between actual and forecast will be a cause of further investigation. The stock returns must also show:

1   How many productive hours were lost by the factory because necessary raw materials were not available
2   How many orders from customers were lost because stocks of finished goods were not on hand
3   The justification for any rise that has been made in the quantity of each kind of stock being held
4   What stocks have not turned over during the period

Where stock turnover has been very low, it may be necessary to inquire whether it should be cleared partially or completely and if so by what means. If there are frequent cases of stock being very slow moving the whole policy of deciding on stocks may need revision as excessive quantities are being put into stock.

The management accounting records will aim to extract the necessary information about the stock with the usual qualifications of speed and accuracy.

Stock Valuation

Figure 10:1 shows the alternative methods available for evaluating stock. When a method of valuation is selected it should be applied consistently year after year.

In view of the big difference the valuation of stock can make to both the profit measurement and the balance sheet, instructions to staff about stock checking and stock valuation should be given clearly to avoid misunderstanding. Essentials for producing accurate results include:

1   The quantity of stock (weight, number, length or whatever unit of measurement) must be listed accurately.
2   The entire stock should be reviewed by the departmental managers or their senior assistants to judge the extent of any deterioration of quality and/or the effect of obsolescence or changes of fashion. Cuts for these reasons should be listed so that their relative importance as an item in arriving at the profit may be judged.
3   Values should be applied to the stock according to the rules set out in Figure 10:1.
4   Where market value is used because it is lower than cost price the amount lost for this reason should be calculated. For example, if cost price would be £1000 but market value is only £900, the profit for the period has been reduced by £100 below whatever would have been the profit in normal trading.
5   The stock valuation fixed for monthly and annual accounts should not be used for price fixing. To calculate a selling price, the cost of buying the materials should be the current figure or, alternatively, the average figure for a period.

6   This stock valuation is not to be used for fire and theft insurance purposes. A separate valuation, at the higher of either actual cost or replacement cost, is needed for this purpose.

7   Value of stock was sometimes based on the facts as they existed on the stock-taking date and no notice taken of subsequent changes in either cost or selling price. For example, if stock at cost price was £10 per unit on stocktaking day or 31 December, Year 1 and, owing to a general collapse of the markets during January, its market value dropped to only £7 per unit by 31 January, Year 2, the December stock would still have been shown at £10 for the trading account of the year ended 31 December, Year 1. The result would be that the company showed a good profit for Year 1 and yet would have achieved less in Year 2 from selling the overpriced materials which it held in stock at the beginning of that year.

This practice would have contravened SSAP 9, referred to later in this chapter, and a practical way of dealing with the problem would be to set up a separate stock provision to include reductions in market value below cost.

8   The purchasing department should be prepared to find the current costs for raw materials as at the stocktaking date by making inquiries from suppliers. They will probably only do this for the main items and estimate the lesser items from the general information available. Instructions to purchasing officers should be issued prior to the accounting date or a standing instruction backed by a reminder should be issued by the managing director a few days before the date. It is likely to be easier to obtain supplies of figures at that time rather than to ask for them back-dated several months later.

9   The selling departments will be similarly involved in finding market values for the finished goods and they too should be encouraged to do this at about the time of the accounting date rather than later.

Stock value in monthly accounts

Unless there are any violent fluctuations in prices, the monthly accounts usually rely on cost without the added complication of finding market values. This is a case of sacrificing full accuracy for the sake of economy. If this policy is kept right through the whole of the accounting year the result may be that the twelve one-monthly accounts will show a larger profit than the final annual accounts when they are prepared, the difference being because of any reduction in market values at the annual accounting date.

As a compromise it is quite possible to bring the stocks on to market valuation twice a year, so that they do not go very far adrift from the normal monthly accounts.

Corrections to stock values

Draft accounts may be prepared using the first quick valuation of the trading stock, then, when the results have been studied in outline, it may be found that the stock value is open to queries and, after careful consideration by the management, fresh figures based on corrected stocks may be prepared. Particular care is needed, for the opening stock value for the following period, to use the correct revised figures from the final versions of the accounts for the period which has just ended and not those from the draft accounts which were incorrect.

Raw material at cost

Where there is a flow of identical material into and out of stock, and it is not practical to find the actual cost of each item in stock at a particular date, there are four common methods for judging the average cost of the present stock. 'First in first out' is the one most generally used and it is preferred by the Inland Revenue. Companies which use one of the other three methods are likely to be required by the Inland Revenue to repeat their calculations using the FIFO method and to revise the profit for corporation tax purposes.

Base stock method is logical and sensible when a permanent base stock must be retained as it is reasonable to assume the value remains unchanged for ever. Indeed, it is possible to query whether this base stock has any real value at all, as the company is unable to sell it as long as it continues in business and it is often ignored in cost accounting. Yet the fact remains that this method was not acceptable to the Inland Revenue which considered that the base stock rose steadily in value over the decades in sympathy with rising replacement costs. This attitude was modified somewhat with the advent of savage inflation.

To mitigate the severe cash flow problems faced by companies as a result of rapid increases in inflation, the Finance Act 1975 introduced stock relief, whereby an increase in stock values in the accounting year did not automatically bring a concomitant increase in the tax liability. A more permanent system was introduced in the 1976 Finance Act, and the 1980 Finance Act brought in deferment of "claw-back" to allow for temporary "dips".

Raw material at market value

As a company is not intended to be in business for the purpose of reselling raw material in its original form, the market value should be the cost price of obtaining fresh supplies of stock on the stocktaking date.

Work in progress at cost

The cost price for work in progress includes:

1   The actual raw material valued on the same basis as the main stock of raw material – plus
2   The direct wages and other direct expenses – plus
3   An amount for overhead expenses

It may be possible to measure the actual amount of direct wages already incurred, in which case this should be done. However, in many firms the work in progress consists of numerous units all at different stages of manufacture.

In this case there is no choice but to make a careful estimate of the overall proportion of work carried out. For example, if completed jobs take four hours it might be considered that work in progress was on average half-made and the wages for two hours per unit should be taken into the valuation. The number of units should be measured carefully as always.

Whether to add something for the value of overheads in the work in progress was almost completely a matter of opinion. It was possible to justify adding any proportion of the overheads from zero to the full amount as for finished goods. In 1975 a Statement of Standard Accounting Practice, SSAP 9, was issued under the title of Stocks and Work in Progress. This included the statement that costs of stocks and work in progress should comprise normal expenditure incurred in bringing the product to its present location and condition. Such costs to include all related production overheads.

Work in progress at market value

Work in progress will not normally be sold in its unfinished state so there is no true market value. However, in circumstances which it is hoped arise only at rare intervals, the final selling price of the product may be lower than the present cost price of the work in progress. This could arise, for example, in building and construction work when work on a single project of high value may continue over a period of several months.

In these circumstances the value should be the selling price minus a reasonable estimate of the costs which still remain to be incurred on the project. The result will be to incorporate the loss on the project in the period just ending and leave the following period to see the completion of the work with neither further loss nor profit. This is a reasonable approach to this problem, because the loss in the past period is quite genuine as this is the time when the unfortunate contract has been created and brought into existence.

Finished goods at cost

This section on finished goods would relate to stocks held by wholesalers and retailers which have been bought ready made from other firms as well as to goods made in a manufacturing company's own factories.

The cost price should be the direct costs plus a full proportionate addition for the overhead expenses. For example, if direct costs are £10 and overheads, other than sales expenses from the profit and loss account, are £12, the stock will be valued at £22. Some companies find reasonable justification for adding a lower percentage to the stock valuation and this is satisfactory provided they are consistent.

Selling costs incurred during a period must apply to the goods already sold and not to the unsold stock, so no addition should be made for these in the stock valuation.

Finished goods at market value

To satisfy the Inland Revenue these stocks should be valued at the selling price minus selling and distribution expenses yet to be incurred. The result will be to have made a loss on these items during the period just ended and to complete the sale of them with neither profit nor loss during the coming period.

Accounting Ratios

The standard ratio for the rate of stock turnover is the cost of goods sold divided by value of stock. For example, if the cost of goods sold is £10 000 and the value of stock is £1000, the rate of stock turnover is ten times. Usually the annual figure is used to find the number of times a year.

This ratio is almost meaningless where there is more than one kind of stock, which includes the majority of all stocks in all companies because it hides the variation in turnover rate for each different line. For example:

Stock of A = £20	Cost of amounts sold £ 40	Rate of turnover 2 times
Stock of B = £20	Cost of amounts sold £200	Rate of turnover 10 times
Total £40	£240	6

Here the rate overall appears to be six times a year, which management might consider a fair average for their kind of trade. But item A is moving too slowly whilst B is moving so rapidly that the stock may well be too small in relation to the demand. Therefore, this ratio is useful only when it is shown for each separate kind of stock.

Stock ratios cannot be used over short periods when the trade is seasonal because either the supply of raw material or the disposal of the final product is concentrated into a few weeks of the year.

Purchasing

The aims of good purchasing are to obtain the correct material in the right quantities at the right time for the most satisfactory price.

The weaknesses which may reflect in the monthly profit figures include:

1   Prices agreed on the orders have been exceeded on the supplier's invoice, or the goods were ordered without a firm price being agreed and the actual price has been higher than had been allowed for in the costing system
2   Deliveries have failed to keep stocks at the required level, perhaps to the point where the factory or warehouse was short of necessary goods

Goods required

1   Estimates of the demand likely to arise, with as much forewarning as possible and with a correct description of the nature, size, style, colour and other specifications of what will be needed
2   The price paid last time for goods of this kind

Goods received

1   The arrival of the goods from suppliers, or more particularly, their non-arrival when they were due
2   Usage of goods from the raw materials warehouse by the factory. In the case of a retailing or wholesaling company, the equivalent is the amount of goods sold
3   Discovery when any goods inwards were not up to standard and must be returned to the supplier and replacements obtained

The following is a list of the routine documents used to initiate some action in purchasing (see also Figure 10:2):

OUTGOING	INCOMING
1 Inquiry – to several possible suppliers	2 Quotations from suppliers
3 Order – to selected supplier	4 Order acknowledgment, goods with advice note from suppliers; despatch note from suppliers; invoice from suppliers

OUTGOING	INCOMING
5 Supplier's invoice to accounts office after checking	

6 Advice note with goods returned
   to supplier
	7 Credit note from
	   supplier

8 Supplier's credit note to accounts office	

In addition there are static documents:

In the office

Copies of inquiries and of orders
Diary system for progress chasing on goods not delivered to time
Card system – card for each material, listing all the normal suppliers and noting them

In the goods inwards warehouse

Goods inwards record – serving as a base for checking supplier's invoices
Stock records – goods in stock
                        goods issued to factory
From warehouse to purchasing office – advice of routine replacement orders needed

Progress chasing

It is also necessary to urge overdue deliveries, and it is useful to keep a continuing record of goods overdue. In many companies a record, such as the one shown in Figure 10:3, is prepared each month showing goods overdue.

Invoice checking

Goods normally arrive with an advice note. If there is no advice note, the warehouseman should make one up. Goods are then checked to see if they are satisfactory and that they tally with the advice note. If the goods are not satisfactory they should be returned to the supplier. Goods which do not tally with the advice note need not be returned.

Goods are then put into a warehouse and the advice note placed in a temporary file. When the invoice arrives it is matched to the advice note and they are stapled together. If an invoice has arrived but there is no advice note, a check should be made to see whether the goods have, in fact, arrived and the advice note been mislaid. If the goods have not arrived, the invoice should be held for no more than three days and then telephone inquiries should be made to the supplier. The supplier should also be sent a written notice of non-arrival of goods.

The invoice should be checked against the order for price, quality, quantity. If an invoice is not in agreement with an order, the company should telephone or write to the supplier and the invoice be held until a correction is received. The invoice should also be checked for arithmetic of extension and addition. If the invoice is inaccurate, the supplier should be sent a letter and the invoice held until a correction is received.

Goods returned to supplier

If goods are either rejected on arrival by the warehouse staff or found to be faulty when they come to be used in the factory, a notice should be sent immediately to the supplier, advising him that the goods are being returned, with copies:

1   To accompany the actual goods
2   To dispatch separately by post to the supplier
3   To retain in the office

In addition a copy should be passed to the firm's own accounts office if the goods have already been accepted and their invoice passed for payment. If the fault is discovered before the invoice has been passed for payment, the copy should be held in the purchasing office and attached to the supplier's invoice.

Correction of discrepancy

Returning goods to suppliers is not the only possible or necessary action when there is a discrepancy in quantity or quality.

Though the goods may be acceptable there may be a mistake in the invoice. A note should be sent to the supplier asking for a correction to the price or quantity shown. The invoice will be retained in the purchasing office awaiting the supplier's credit note. It may be necessary to ask the supplier to send the correct items, even though the incorrect ones are being kept. A telephone call and written confirmation is usually the best approach to this.

	VALUE OF STOCK IS THE LOWER OF —		
	COST PRICE	OR	MARKET VALUE
Raw material	(*a*) Actual cost if items are individually identifiable (*b*) First in first out (*c*) Last in first out (*d*) Weighted average cost (*e*) Base stock method		(*a*) Cost to purchase some more at stocktaking date (*b*) Price obtainable by re-selling at this date (not a satisfactory method)
Work in progress	(*a*) Actual cost of raw material and direct wages (*b*) As in (*a*) but plus a proportion of overhead costs (*c*) As in (*a*) but plus full amount of overheads		Not applicable unless it is known that finished products are being sold below the cost already calculated in the cost price column then take selling price minus inevitable expenses yet to be incurred
Finished goods	(*a*) Actual cost individually calculated including share of overheads (*b*) Cost of most recent production (*c*) Average cost of production through the period Query—amount to be included for overheads		(*a*) Selling price (*b*) Selling price minus selling and other costs yet to be incurred (*c*) Selling price minus selling and other costs minus **a margin for profit** to be made when the sale is effected (not satisfactory to Revenue)
Spoiled goods	Not applicable		Deterioration through rust, corrosion or similar physical faults to be assessed on their merits to find probable selling price, from which costs may be deducted
Goods unsold through obsolescence or change of fashion			Assess the anticipated selling price for out of fashion or obsolete goods and deduct costs to be incurred

Figure 10:1   Stock valuation — choice of methods

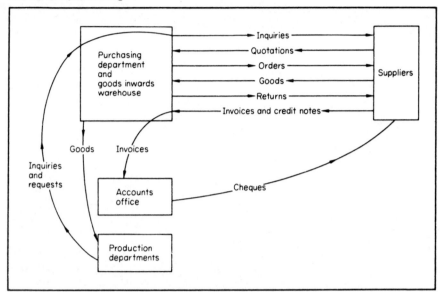

Figure 10:2   Purchasing patterns

					Date_____		
Date due	Supplier	Description of goods	Date(s) of reminders issued	Revised date promised by supplier	Degree of urgency	User— department notified	
15 Mar	Smith	40 units K2RB	15 Mar, 28 Mar	10 April	Not important	Department *AB*	
22 Feb	Brown	80 units M4ZA	22 Feb, 6,14,21,28 Mar	15 April	Desperate	Department *CD*	
					Moderate		

Figure 10:3   Record of goods overdue

Index